RaphaelJS
Graphics and Visualization on the Web

Chris Wilson

Beijing · Cambridge · Farnham · Köln · Sebastopol · Tokyo

RaphaelJS

by Chris Wilson

Printed in the United States of America.

Published by O'Reilly Media, Inc., 1005 Gravenstein Highway North, Sebastopol, CA 95472.

O'Reilly books may be purchased for educational, business, or sales promotional use. Online editions are also available for most titles (*http://my.safaribooksonline.com*). For more information, contact our corporate/institutional sales department: 800-998-9938 or *corporate@oreilly.com*.

Editors: Simon St. Laurent and Allyson MacDonald	**Interior Designer:** David Futato
Production Editor: Nicole Shelby	**Illustrator:** Rebecca Demarest
Cover Designer: Randy Comer	

December 2013:   First Edition

Revision History for the First Edition:

2013-12-09:   First release

See *http://oreilly.com/catalog/errata.csp?isbn=9781449365363* for release details.

ISBN: 978-1-449-36536-3

[LSI]

Table of Contents

Preface

I once heard programming described as a way to "express your ideas through a computer." To me, that morsel of wisdom encapsulates everything that is wonderful and awful about writing code: it gives us the vocabulary to work through our ideas and then lays bare the limits of our ingenuity.

If everyone had the same sorts of ideas, we would only need one programming language. The quotation above comes from a book about Ruby, which many people will fervently argue is the finest language around (often long after you would have preferred to change the subject).

But of course, people have all sorts of wild ideas that cannot be properly served by one language. This book, which is about the JavaScript library called Raphael, is for a specific subset of human ideas: visual ones.

If you're a person who thinks visually and wants to learn to code, there's a good chance you've been frustrated by efforts to learn classical programming languages like Ruby, Python, PHP, or even JavaScript itself, the programming language that is embedded in every web browser. Most tutorials tend to start you out with printing words to the screen, writing functions to print more words to the screen, and, if you're lucky, maybe branching into printing numbers to the screen by the end of the first lesson.

In *RaphaelJS*, we'll be painting the screen with all manner of shapes and colors, animating them through space and time, and bending them to our will (via the tyranny of our mouse and fingers). Every example and lesson in this book runs in the browser and is 100% web-ready, meaning you can upload it directly to your site to have living, breathing visuals that run in any browser.

While this book is not explicitly an introduction to JavaScript, I've done my best to make it accessible to people who are new to the field. None of the code in this book requires advanced mastery of computer science or a deep foundational understanding of JavaScript. It is meant to get both new and experienced coders up and running as fast as possible.

The only tool we need for this book, besides a computer, is the Raphael.js library, which is open-source and freely available at RaphaelJS.com under the MIT License. Bringing a few visual ideas to the table won't hurt, either. By the end of this manual, you'll be ready to express them in code.

Conventions Used in This Book

The following typographical conventions are used in this book:

Italic
    Indicates new terms, URLs, email addresses, filenames, and file extensions.

`Constant width`
    Used for program listings, as well as within paragraphs to refer to program elements such as variable or function names, databases, data types, environment variables, statements, and keywords.

`Constant width bold`
    Shows commands or other text that should be typed literally by the user.

`Constant width italic`
    Shows text that should be replaced with user-supplied values or by values determined by context.

 This icon signifies a tip, suggestion, or general note.

 This icon indicates a warning or caution.

Using Code Examples

Supplemental material (code examples, exercises, etc.) is available for download at *http://jsfiddle.net/user/raphaeljs/fiddles*.

This book is here to help you get your job done. In general, if example code is offered with this book, you may use it in your programs and documentation. You do not need to contact us for permission unless you're reproducing a significant portion of the code. For example, writing a program that uses several chunks of code from this book does not require permission. Selling or distributing a CD-ROM of examples from O'Reilly books does require permission. Answering a question by citing this book and quoting example code does not require permission. Incorporating a significant amount of example code from this book into your product's documentation does require permission.

We appreciate, but do not require, attribution. An attribution usually includes the title, author, publisher, and ISBN. For example: "*RaphaelJS* by Chris Wilson (O'Reilly). Copyright 2014 Chris Wilson, 978-1-449-36536-3."

If you feel your use of code examples falls outside fair use or the permission given above, feel free to contact us at *permissions@oreilly.com*.

Safari® Books Online

 Safari Books Online is an on-demand digital library that delivers expert content in both book and video form from the world's leading authors in technology and business.

Technology professionals, software developers, web designers, and business and creative professionals use Safari Books Online as their primary resource for research, problem solving, learning, and certification training.

Safari Books Online offers a range of product mixes and pricing programs for organizations, government agencies, and individuals. Subscribers have access to thousands of books, training videos, and prepublication manuscripts in one fully searchable database from publishers like O'Reilly Media, Prentice Hall Professional, Addison-Wesley Professional, Microsoft Press, Sams, Que, Peachpit Press, Focal Press, Cisco Press, John Wiley & Sons, Syngress, Morgan Kaufmann, IBM Redbooks, Packt, Adobe Press, FT Press, Apress, Manning, New Riders, McGraw-Hill, Jones & Bartlett, Course Technology, and dozens more. For more information about Safari Books Online, please visit us online.

How to Contact Us

Please address comments and questions concerning this book to the publisher:

O'Reilly Media, Inc.
1005 Gravenstein Highway North
Sebastopol, CA 95472
800-998-9938 (in the United States or Canada)
707-829-0515 (international or local)
707-829-0104 (fax)

We have a web page for this book, where we list errata, examples, and any additional information. You can access this page at *http://oreil.ly/raphael-js*.

To comment or ask technical questions about this book, send email to *bookques tions@oreilly.com.*

For more information about our books, courses, conferences, and news, see our website at *http://www.oreilly.com.*

Find us on Facebook: *http://facebook.com/oreilly*

Follow us on Twitter: *http://twitter.com/oreillymedia*

Watch us on YouTube: *http://www.youtube.com/oreillymedia*

Acknowledgments

First and foremost, I would like to thank my wife Susan, who always dreamed that someday her husband would write her a book on JavaScript visualization.

We are all indebted to Dmitry Baranovskiy, the inventive force behind the Raphael library, and to the dozens of others who have contributed ideas and fixes. Dmitry truly led the charge in uniting the divergent drawing technologies on the Web, making all of the wonderful visuals we enjoy online today possible.

I'm indebted, of course, to my crack team of editors at O'Reilly: Simon St. Laurent, Meghan Blanchette, and Allyson MacDonald. And a special thanks to Gretchen Giles, whose response to my tweet wondering whether O'Reilly authors get to pick the woodcut on their covers kicked off this whole process. They do not, but I couldn't be happier with the Nile Valley Sunbird.

CHAPTER 1

Introduction: Why Raphael is Great

Raphael is a toolkit for making beautiful things on the Web. With a few lines of code and the help of a small, free JavaScript library, you can turn the browser into a living gallery of interactive artwork and visualization. This book will teach you how to bridge the gulf between the page and your imagination.

Let's dive straight into a complete working example.

```
<!DOCTYPE html>
<html>
    <head>
        <title>Red dot</title>
    </head>
    <body>
        <div id="container"></div>
            <script  src="http://cdnjs.cloudflare.com/ajax/libs/raphael/2.1.0/
raphael-min.js"></script>
        <script>
var paper = Raphael("container", 500, 300);
var dot = paper.circle(250, 150, 100).attr({
    fill: "#FF0000",
    stroke: "#000099",
    "stroke-width": 3
});
        </script>
    </body>
</html>
```

Load this code into any browser—either by hand or on a site like jsFiddle (*http://jsFiddle.net*) that lets you experiment with code—and with any luck, you will see this:

See this code live on jsFiddle (*http://jsfiddle.net/raphaeljs/rqvtB/*).

If you're not impressed yet, don't worry. You've actually seen something pretty neat. Let's go over what we just did:

- We took a bare bones HTML page and added a single `<div>` element with the id `container`.

- We loaded a small JavaScript library named raphael-min.js, which clocks in at 89Kb, hosted on CloudFlare (*http://www.cloudflare.com*).

- We wrote two lines of JavaScript: one that initializes Raphael, and a second that gives the command to make a dot at the coordinates 250, 150 with a radius of 100 pixels. Then we made the dot red with a blue border (or *stroke*) 3 pixels in width.

What excites me most about Raphael is that it is not just about drawing, but about writing commands that instruct the browser to draw something a specific way when the user loads your web page. As we will see, the browser has prodigious artistic talents if you offer it the proper guidance.

Best of all, Raphael works on nearly every browser, including old ones like Internet Explorer 7 and 8, which plenty of people still use. (As much as we all wish this was not the case, this is still a legitimate concern for anyone wishing to reach a wide audience.) Raphael does not require any external plug-ins like Flash or Java, making it much friendlier for mobile devices. If you want to ensure that as many people as possible see your work, there is currently no better solution than Raphael for interactive visualizations.

This book will take you from that modest red dot to lively, interactive graphics and visualizations in just a few chapters, no matter where you're coming from or how much you do or don't know about the Web. And we'll have a good time doing it.

Inside Every Browser, an Artist

I am always a bit puzzled when people talk about data visualization as though it's a new frontier on the Web, because in some sense everything on the Web is a data visualization. Whether you are hand-coding files for your Harry Potter fan fiction site, dreaming up a video game that runs in the browser, or relaunching a major website for your company, your job is to take a lot of information and present it to your users in a way that is easy to understand and (ideally) not too horrible to look at.

To accomplish this, you enlist the services of the three-headed deity of the Internet: HTML, CSS and JavaScript. I like to think of this troika as the body, clothing, and personality of the Web: HTML (HyperText Markup Language) creates *things*—boxes, paragraphs, tables, buttons—CSS (cascading style sheets) controls the *appearance* of these things—color, font, positioning—and JavaScript controls their *behavior*—what happens when the user clicks on this or mouses over that.

All Web development consists of writing instructions for a program—the browser—to interpret and assemble into a data visualization, even if that visualization is as simple as some black words against a white background. This can be a maddening process, since not everyone uses the same browser for the assembly process, and because no two browsers fully agree on what the final product should look like. But on the whole, I think the browser is one of the most underappreciated strokes of genius in recent human history. Visual information is no longer produced by an artist or designer, copied a bunch of times, and then distributed to customers. Instead, it is transmitted as a series of instructions and put together on the spot. It's as if, instead of offering a book of famous paintings, your local bookstore offered you the paint itself and some very precise instructions on how to produce *The School of Athens*.

This would be a stupid way to distribute great masterpieces, but it is a brilliant way to transmit web pages. Computers are much better at following instructions than you are and much faster at doing it, and a set instructions—that is, code—is much easier to transmit than the final product. On top of that, computers are animated and responsive. The fellows and ladies in *The School of Athens* will not respond no matter how many times you poke and prod them before Vatican security hunts you down. Computer visualizations, by contrast, can morph and transform on demand, like photographs in *Harry Potter*. Raphael is the toolkit that allows you to breathe magic and life into images that you create.

Why Raphael?

There are a few different Web-based technologies you can use for interactive visuals online, from the rapidly aging Flash platform to those that take advantage of the adolescent HTML5 `<canvas>` element. I see three main reasons to use Raphael:

It's easy

Raphael is written entirely in JavaScript, the native language of the Web. JavaScript is a glorious language whose supreme friendliness to inexperienced developers more than compensates for a few design flaws. If you're new to the world of Web development, Raphael is an excellent place to start because you will immediately be able to see the fruits of your efforts right there on the screen. If you have experience with any aspect of webpage design, Raphael will make immediate, intuitive sense. Unlike many (worthy) HTML5 technologies, it will not require rewiring your mind or learning an entirely different approach to design.

It's popular

You shouldn't use Raphael just because everyone else is, but it's nice to know you're not alone. Every day, I see new questions about Raphael on the indespensible forum Stack Overflow (*http://www.stackoverflow.com*), where coders pose and answer each other's questions. Almost every one is answered satisfactorily within hours (sometimes by me). Like all good JavaScript libraries, it's open-source, meaning veteran users can sift through the source code to resolve even the knottiest problems.

It works

Under the hood, as they say, Raphael uses a format known as Scalable Vector Graphics (SVG), the browser's built-in graphics language. For older versions of Internet Explorer that do not speak SVG, it "falls back" on a similar format known as Vector Markup Language (VML). By contrast, popular visualization tools like D3JS and ProcessingJS do not work on older browsers. At the time of this writing, just under 15% (*http://www.w3counter.com/globalstats.php*) of users worldwide have a version of Internet Explorer earlier than IE9, meaning they would see a blank screen if you use one of those tools. That number will be higher or lower depending on the demographics of your audience, and it will continue to recede worldwide each year, but the added compatibility is a nice check mark in Raphael's column.

Because the drawing tools are native to browsers, Raphael does not require any plugins or other third-party tools either to view or to compose. All you need is a browser and a text editor.

If you're interested in how SVG works, O'Reilly publishes an *SVG Essentials* (*http://oreil.ly/svg-essentials*) guide that's worth the price just for the picture of the great argus pheasant on the front. If, like me, you're not that interested, that's fine too. The beauty of Raphael is that it takes care of all of the drawing behind the scenes.

What About D3.js? I've Heard It's Better for Web Visualizations

D3, which stands for "data-driven documents," is a fantastic JavaScript library written by Mike Bostock, one of the leading visionaries in browser-based data visualization. As its name suggests, it specializes in quickly translating raw datasets into visualizations, from Microsoft Excel-style charts and graphs to social network diagrams and sunburst diagrams. If your goal is to make interactive charts and graphs based on large datasets, and if you're already a confident JavaScript programmer, D3 might be the right place to start.

But there's a reason I'm writing a book about Raphael and not D3—besides the fact that O'Reilly already has a book on D3. Data visualization is a small subset of the sort of imaginative visuals that JavaScript and SVG are capable of.

Raphael is also considerably easier to learn. At work, I use D3 for projects that specifically call for it, and Raphael for everything else. (D3 also does not work on Internet Explorer 8 and below, unlike Raphael. Learning Raphael will also give you a keen familiarity with the standard properties of SVG objects, which will come in handy if you decide to give D3 a try later on.

One reason I like SVG graphics is that they are an extremely natural extension of HTML. A square in SVG is represented by a tag on the page, just like an image or a paragraph. You can style your shapes with CSS the same way you would anything else. This stands in contrast to the HTML5 `<canvas>` object, which introduces a new capability for drawing images in the browser. The `<canvas>` is capable of more sophisticated computer graphics than SVG, but it is also more of a divergence in concept and coding strategy. I would use it for an involved in-browser video game or a heavy duty animation, but I would stick to SVG for everything else.

I'm Convinced. Let's Get Started.

I thought you'd never ask! Just a few housekeeping notes:

Like any good JavaScript developer, I follow the sage advice of Douglas Crockford, a longtime evangelist for the language and author of the indispensible JavaScript: The Good Parts (*http://oreil.ly/java-good-parts*), a book I promise I would recommend even if I weren't writing this book for the same publisher. JavaScript is flexible enough that there are usually many ways to accomplish the same task, and Crockford has very good ideas about which approach to take.

While all of my examples with follow his guidelines, I do not care how you write your code. I get very frustrated when I see experienced programmers lecturing greenhorns on best practices when the newcomer has just begun learning a language or a new toolset.

Conventions exist to help experienced developers stay organized and avoid errors, not to sap all the fun out of experimenting with a new skill set. So have at it, however you like.

As for how to follow along in this book, you'll simply be loading a text file of commands —a web page—into a browser. Everything Raphael does is "client side," meaning it runs on the user's machine, not on a server somewhere. So you do not need an elaborate development environment, just a way to load your code into a browser. This can be as simple as editing a document with Notepad and loading it in a browser from your desktop, though you ought to do yourself a favor and get a text editor that recognizes code and highlights it in different colors for your viewing convenience. I recommend Notepad++ for PCs and TextWrangler for Mac. Or you can skip all of that and go to a site like jsFiddle (*http://jsFiddle.net*) or jsBin (*http://www.jsBin.com*), both of which allow you to paste code into a window and see it come alive right there on the page. It doesn't really matter, so long as the beautiful things you will create find their way to the screen.

CHAPTER 2

Shapes

In the introduction, we looked at a complete working example of Raphael that drew a red dot on the page. Since Raphael is a fundamentally visual toolkit, this will take the place of the canonical "Hello World" example in the first chapter of programming books since time immemorial.

In case, like me, you never read the introduction, here it is again.

```
<!DOCTYPE html>
<html>
    <head>
        <title>Red dot</title>
    </head>
    <body>
        <div id="container"></div>
            <script  src="http://cdnjs.cloudflare.com/ajax/libs/raphael/2.1.0/
raphael-min.js"></script>
        <script>
var paper = Raphael("container", 500, 300);
var dot = paper.circle(250, 150, 100).attr({
    fill: "#FF0000",
    stroke: "#000099",
    "stroke-width": 3
});
        </script>
    </body>
</html>
```

See this code live on jsFiddle (*http://jsfiddle.net/raphaeljs/rqvtB/*).

Let's do a deep dive into this example.

Getting Raphael

Like jQuery, Google Maps, Backbone, or any other JavaScript library, Raphael is neatly packed in a single external library that you include in your webpage with a `<script>` tag:

```
<script src="http://cdnjs.cloudflare.com/ajax/libs/raphael/2.1.0/raphael-min.js"></script>
```

CloudFlare is a cloud services company that generously provides a free CDN, or "content delivery network," for fast, highly available access to Raphael (and many other JavaScript libraries). I'm using it here because it prevents me from needing to say things like "first download the Raphael script, then put it in same folder as your HTML page." You can either continue using the file on CloudFlare or host the file yourself—whatever you prefer.

As of this writing, the most recent release of Raphael is 2.1.2. (CloudFlare is a tiny bit behind here.) That will change, but it is unlikely that examples you create in this version will break as new versions come out with new features. Or if you want to practice on jsFiddle (*http://jsFiddle.net*), you can include Raphael from the list of available JavaScript libraries.

Initializing Raphael

Once this library is included in a page, you'll have access to a JavaScript object intuitively named Raphael, from which all the wonderful capabilities of the toolkit extend. Your first task in any project is to tell the library where on your page you would like to start drawing:

```
var paper = Raphael("container", 500, 300);
```

The first argument in the function `Raphael()` is the id of the HTML element inside of which you'd like to start drawing things. You can pass a variety of elements, but in general a `<div>` will suit our needs wonderfully. The important point is that Raphael operates inside the cosmos of individual elements on the page. We're going to cover the ways in which it integrates nicely with the rest of a web page, but to start, you should think of this `<div>` element as a blank canvas.

The next two arguments give the width and height of that canvas, which of course depend on how much you plan to draw. In relation to what else you've got going on on the page, it may be wise to explicitly set the element containing our canvas to the same dimensions. Otherwise, the `<div>` will dynamically resize to contain the new canvas.

Under the hood, declaring a `Raphael()` object will place a new element on the web page inside the element you chose to contain the whole project. This is the `<svg>` element that will contain everything else we create. It's useful to remember that as we make circles, lines, pictures, and everything else, Raphael is taking our JavaScript commands and using them to create new objects on the screen. But one of the great joys of Raphael is that you don't have to worry about this too much—it's all taken care of. In fact, you can go ahead and smash the "<" and ">" keys on your keyboard, because we have freed ourselves of the need to write tags directly.

(Actually, scratch that, you may need them for "less than" and "greater than." But you get the idea.)

The `Raphael()` function is actually quite flexible, and offers several other options for creating canvases, including generating its own HTML element to contain itself and appending it to the web page. (This is useful for situations like bookmarklets, where you're writing JavaScript to execute on someone else's page.) You can see all the possibilities on the documentation page (*http://raphaeljs.com/reference.html#Raphael*).

I won't waste valuable paper/pixels declaring a `var paper` object for every example in this book, but creating it is an essential first step to every project. And while you can name the Raphael object anything you like, almost every example you'll see anywhere names it `paper`. So I will too.

And you should bookmark that URL to the Raphael documentation. We're going to be coming back to it a lot.

Drawing Things

The `paper` object we just declared contains most of the tools we need to make beauty on the Web. That includes the circle function, which takes three arguments: the x and y values of the center of the circle and its radius, like so:

```
var dot = paper.circle(250, 150, 100);
```

Simple enough, right? If you run this code, you should see an empty circle with a thin black border.

Let's not be content with so bland a drawing. To give the circle a fill color and a stronger border, we can assign it attributes, like these:

```
dot.attr("fill", "red");
dot.attr("stroke", "blue");
dot.attr("stroke-width", 3);
```

You can achieve the exact same effect in one line, like this:

```
dot.attr({
    fill: "red",
    stroke: "blue",
    "stroke-width": 3
});
```

If you're new to JavaScript, the former method, while more verbose, will be easier to decipher. If you're confused about when you do and don't need quotation marks, you'll want to beef up on "JavaScript Object Notation," or JSON. We'll be seeing him again.

Okay, so now we have a beautiful blue-encrusted red dot on the page. Let's take a quick tour of the other shapes Raphael can make.

Basic Shapes

In addition to circles, Raphael has the built-in cability of drawing ellipses and rectangles. The former is exactly like the `.circle()` method, but takes four inputs instead of three: the x and y values of the center and two radii, one vertical and one horizontal:

```
var ell = paper.ellipse(100, 100, 50, 20);
```

The `.rect()` function takes the same four arguments and makes a rectangle:

```
var rec = paper.rect(100, 100, 50, 20);
```

Let's try them at the same time, with a little color:

```
var ell = paper.ellipse(100, 100, 50, 20).attr("fill", "orange");
var rec = paper.rect(100, 100, 50, 20).attr("fill", "green");
```

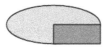

Wait a minute—if we entered the exact same numbers into the two shape functions, why is the rectangle so much smaller? It's because the shapes interpret the inputs differently. To an ellipse, the first two arguments refer to the center of the shape and the following two numbers refer to the radii. For a rectangle, the x and y coordinates refer to the location of the upper-left corner, while the next two numbers refer to the length of the side.

Notice also that the rectangle appears on top of the ellipse. This is because the command to draw it occurs after the one to draw the ellipse. Unlike the "z-index" property of CSS, which determines which elements appear above or below others, Raphael draws things in the order you ask it to, painting over existing elements when there's overlap. There are ways to manipulate this, but you should understand how it works by default.

Images

Like regular HTML, Raphael can load image files. While this may seem redundant, if you're using an image as part of a larger drawing then you will be much, much happier loading it in Raphael than the old-fashioned way.

```
var fluffy = paper.image("mydog.png", 25, 20, 120, 100);
```

This will cause the script to look in the local directory for an image called "mydog.png" and place it on the canvas with the upper-left corner at the coordinates (25,20) with a width of 120 pixels and a height of 100 pixels, just like the syntax for a rectangle. Like a regular <img> tag, you can feed the function relative paths ("../img/mydog.png") or the full url to the image. Unlike an <img> tag, you have to specify the dimensions—Raphael will not fall back on the native dimensions of the image.

With that limitation, it would be reasonable to ask why you would bother loading images in Raphael instead of simply placing them on the page with an <img> tag. When combining photos with other drawing objects like lines and shapes—perhaps you're making a chart that shows how various people are connected in a network—the case for SVG images is fairly obvious. But I would actually use Raphael for any diagram of images that requires placing them at different coordinates on a page, even if I didn't need to draw anything else. This is because Raphael has a very simple Cartesian coordinate system, with 0,0 in the upper-left corner. The HTML document, meanwhile, has a much more complex set of rules for positioning elements based on the arrangement of parent containers, the CSS rules for each of those containers, and the model of the browser. You'll save yourself a lot of tedium by loading images in Raphael when you need them in some sort of diagram.

And of course, you're not limited to PNGs. Raphael accepts the same types as a regular web page—JPG, GIF, etc.

Text

To place text on the page, use the `.text()` method. I'm going to get ahead and pre-emptively make the font size large enough to read on the page.

```
var paper = Raphael(0, 0, 500, 200);
var goodnews = paper.text(200, 20, "I bought five copies of
RaphaelJS!").attr("font-size", 16);
var rec = paper.rect(200, 40, 100, 5).attr({ fill: "#CCF", "stroke-width": 0 });
```

I bought five copies of RaphaelJS!

Wait a second. Why is the rectangle, which I added as a reference point, at the center of the text when we fed both items the same coordinates? By default, text objects in Raphael are centered. If you want good old-fashioned left-aligned text, you can specify as much in the attributes. Let's go ahead and change the font while we're in there, and try a 12px font on for size.

```
var paper = Raphael(0, 0, 500, 200);
var rec = paper.rect(200, 40, 100, 5).attr({ fill: "#CCF", "stroke-width": 0 });
var message = "I bought TEN copies of RaphaelJS!"
var betternews = paper.text(200, 20, message).attr({
    "text-anchor": "start",
    "font-size": 12, //in pixels
    "font-family": "Courier New"
});
```

I bought TEN copies of RaphaelJS!

The `text-anchor` attribute is `middle` by default, and can also be set to `end` for right-justified text.

The SVG `text` element is not as flexible as text inside an HTML object. Unlike placing text inside a fixed-width `<div>` element, which will take care of making new lines when the text runs longer than its container, you have to specify line breaks manually here by inserting \n in the text itself where you want the break to occur. While this can be annoying, you generally want to have exact control over where the text appears on the page and when it breaks onto a new line.

For cases where you don't really want to deal with this, we'll cover how to borrow a regular HTML element and insert it seamlessly into your drawing. This is one of the beauties of Raphael—it plays very nicely with its big siblings.

 Most examples that we'll look at in this book involve a single paper object, but there's no reason you can't make as many canvases as you want at different parts of the page. Just remember that each element belongs to one (and only one) canvas.

Attributes

We've now seen several examples where we've made a shape and then specified some attributes like fill color, stroke (outline) width, and font size.

Attributes are not limited to this sort of superficial styling. When you create a new rectangle, the coordinates and radius you choose become attributes as well. In the same way that you can *set* an attribute by passing two values to the .attr() method, you can *get* the current value just by passing the name of the attribute you're curious about.

```
var bestnews = paper.text(200, 20, "I bought fifty copies of RaphaelJS!");
console.log(bestnews.attr("x"));
```

If you go to the developer tools and check out the console—the place where programmers can instruct the program to output messages for reference that the user never sees —you'll see that it has spit out 200.

Likewise, you can set the x coordinate after making a new rectangle:

```
var rec = paper.rect(200, 20, 40, 40);
rec.attr("x", 100);
```

This will place the rectangle at the coordinates (100, 20) immediately after it's made (you'll never see it move). Why not just make it 100 to begin with? Down the line, we'll be making dynamic, responsive animations in which shapes begin life at one location and move after some event triggers them, like a click of the mouse.

It's worth a few minutes to browse all of the available attributes (*http://bit.ly/raphael-reference*) that Raphael offers in the documentation. Of course, not all apply to every object. You can set the font-size of your circles to whatever you like without much effect. And there are a few idiosyncrasies: the .circle() and .ellipse() methods use cx and cy as the attributes representing the center coordinates, not x and y. The appropriate names of the relevant attributes are always specificied in the documentation for that particular method.

Transformations

There is one attribute, `transform`, that deserves special attention because of its importance and its trickiness. This is a versatile property that can manipulate an object in three ways: rotation, translation, and scale.

Let's begin with a set of three rectangles of different colors:

```
var paper = Raphael(0,0,300,300);
var r1 = paper.rect(20, 20, 80, 40).attr("fill", "red");
var r2 = paper.rect(100, 20, 80, 40).attr("fill", "blue");
var r3 = paper.rect(180, 20, 80, 40).attr("fill", "green");
```

Transformations consist of strings with a letter—R, S, or T—followed by some numbers. To rotate an object by 45 degrees, for example, we say:

```
r2.attr("transform", "R45");
```

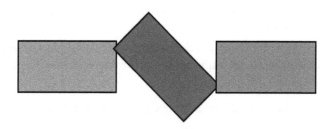

Easy enough. By default, the `transform` property rotates an object around its center. You don't always want this. To specify a different anchor point around which to rotate, pass two more numbers for the coordinates of this point. Here, for example, I am rotating the green rectangle by 90 degrees using the center of the *blue* rectangle as the anchor point. (To better understand how it works, I've added a shaded version of the old rectangle there and drawn a dotted line showing the path of the rotation.)

```
r3.attr("transform", "R90,140,60");
```

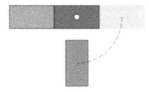

I've added a dotted path here and a yellow dot for the anchor point, just for reference.

Likewise, scaling takes two numbers—the ratio of scaling on the x and y axes—and translation takes two for the number of pixels on the horizontal and vertical axis that you would like to move the object:

```
r1.attr("transform", "T50,60");
r2.attr("transform", "S0.8,0.5")
```

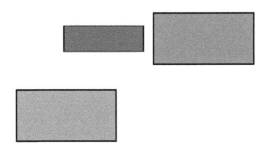

To remove all the transformations and return the shapes to their original state, one would just add the line:

```
r1.attr("transform", "");
```

It's important to understand here that adding a transformation to a shape does *not* alter the values of the original attributes. We can see this very easily here:

```
var paper = Raphael(0, 0, 500, 500);
var r = paper.rect(50, 50, 100, 20);
r.attr("transform", "T30,25");
console.log(r.attr("x"));
```

If you check the output of the console, you will see that the x attribute of the rectangle is still reported as 50, even though the transformation moved the entire shape over to position (80,75). Transformations act on top of the original coordinates, not by modifying the original values.

These basic transformations are pretty straightforward. Where they get tricky is when you start combining them or overriding them with new transformations, but we're not going to get into that just yet.

In the meantime, you may be wondering: What's the point of scaling or translating my shapes, when I could just change the size and coordinates using my newfound mastery of attributes?

Good question. You could absolutely do this. But as our animations and infographics become more complex, we will repeatedly see situations where transformations are a much easier and cleaner way to manipulate our objects. In fact, here's an example right now, in a concept known as…

Sets

There are many situations where objects on the screen are visually related to one another. It is often useful to be able manipulate the elements of all of these visual cousins in one swoop.

Consider the following visualization, which you might see in a children's book of logic problems:

```
var paper = Raphael(0, 0, 500, 500);

//red row
var r1 = paper.rect(25, 25, 50, 50).attr({ 'stroke-width': 0, fill: 'red' });
var r2 = paper.circle(125, 50, 25).attr({ 'stroke-width': 0, fill: 'red' });
var r3 = paper.text(200, 50, "H").attr({
    'stroke-width': 0,
    fill: 'red',
    'font-size': 60
});

//green row
var g1 = paper.rect(100, 100, 50, 50).attr({ 'stroke-width': 0, fill:
'green' });
var g2 = paper.circle(200, 125, 25).attr({ 'stroke-width': 0, fill: 'green' });
var g3 = paper.text(50, 125, "H").attr({
    'stroke-width': 0,
    fill: 'green',
    'font-size': 60
});

//blue row
```

```
var b1 = paper.rect(175, 175, 50, 50).attr({ 'stroke-width': 0, fill: 'blue' });
var b2 = paper.circle(50, 200, 25).attr({ 'stroke-width': 0, fill: 'blue' });

//blank
var blank = paper.text(125, 200, "?").attr({
    'stroke-width': 0,
    fill: 'gray',
    'font-size': 60
});
```

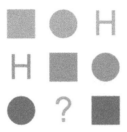

That's all fine and good, but it's a lot of tedious coding. And if we're generating it dynamically, we might as well allow ourselves to vary the pattern—you know those kids are going to try and cheat.

To start, let's get rid of those redundant attribute calls. To do so, we're going to use the .set() method to group our objects by color and then paint them all at once.

```
var paper = Raphael(0, 0, 500, 500);

var r1 = paper.rect(25, 25, 50, 50);
var r2 = paper.circle(125, 50, 25);
var r3 = paper.text(200, 50, "H").attr("font-size", "60px");

var g1 = paper.rect(100, 100, 50, 50);
var g2 = paper.circle(200, 125, 25);
var g3 = paper.text(50, 125, "H").attr("font-size", "60px");

var b1 = paper.rect(175, 175, 50, 50);
var b2 = paper.circle(50, 200, 25);
var b3 = paper.text(125, 200, "?").attr("font-size", "60px");

var red_group = paper.set();
red_group.push(r1, r2, r3);
red_group.attr("fill", "red");

var green_group = paper.set(g1, g2, g3);
green_group.attr("fill", "green");

var blue_group = paper.set(b1, b2, b3).attr("fill", "blue");

b3.attr("fill", "gray");
```

See this code live on jsFiddle (*http://jsfiddle.net/raphaeljs/g4j2c/*).

You'll notice my set declarations got increasingly more compact each time as I condensed the syntax. Once you get the hang of Raphael, you'll be able to save a lot of space by declaring elements and sets and adding attributes all at once, as I did with `blue_group`. But the verbose way is just fine, too. If you've hung around with JavaScript before, you'll probably recognize the `.push()` method for adding elements to sets, which is identical to adding objects to arrays.

Sets operate like arrays in many ways for a simple reason: Under the hood, they *are* arrays, dressed up with some very handy methods for manipulating all the members of the array at once. If you were to output a set directly to the console using `console.log`, you would see the array itself along with some built-in functions. Nothing is preventing you from manipulating this array directly save for one thing: my wagging finger. Generally speaking, you're asking for trouble if you circumvent the Raphael methods and go straight to the internal structure of an object. But it's nice to know it's an option for advanced users when you discover that there is no built-in method for something you'd like to do. Unlike many more rigid languages, JavaScript doesn't automatically erect high walls around the internal cogs of an object.

Okay, fire off the code above and we'll see that we're getting there:

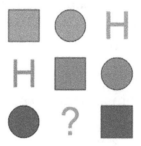

To get the text size where we want it, we'll make a new set of just the text elements. And to eradicate the blue, 1-pixel strokes that appear by default, we'll make a set of the first three sets that encompasses everything:

```
var text_group = paper.set(r3, g3, b3).attr("font-size", 60);
var all_groups = paper.set(red_group, blue_group, green_group).attr("stroke-
width", 0);
```

Once you've run that, you'll see we're back to where we started.

A few important things to note here: Elements can belong to multiple sets, as you see here with the `r3` element, which receives attributes from both `red_group` and `text_group`.

If we were to add a new element to `red_group` at the end of this little program, we might expect it to be (you guessed it) red. Let's try adding a square to the end of the script:

```
red_group.push(paper.rect(300, 25, 50, 50));
```

Bummer. What gives? When you add an attribute to a set in Raphael, it applies those attributes to whatever objects are contained in the set at that time, and has no purchase on what may happen in the future. To make that new square red, we'd have to do so manually or just apply the red fill attribute to the entire set again.

If you're familiar with SVG terminology at all, you might think the Raphael `.set()` method creates a group tag, `<g>`, in the DOM, at which point we would expect new members of the set to assume the attributes of the set added previously. It does not. Sets exist only virtually to connect objects that have something in common. Any method that can be performed on a regular Raphael object, like changing the color or moving it, can be performed on a set of objects as well.

I promised that this section would have something to do with transformations. Let's say we need to move this whole operation 150 pixels to the right. Let's further suppose you read ahead in the Raphael documentation, and noticed that you can access the individual elements in a set of items the same way you would in an array.

We can't just set the x value of each object to 150, since we need to add 150 to its existing value. So you might do this:

```
//loop through the all_groups set
for (var c = 0; c < all_groups.length; c += 1) {
    // loop through the child sets (red_group, blue_group, green_group)
    for (var i = 0; i < all_groups[c].length; i += 1) {
        all_groups[c][i].attr("x", all_groups[c][i].attr("x") + 150);
    }
}
```

Besides being laborious, and besides defeating the purpose of sets altogether, *it doesn't work.* See for yourself:

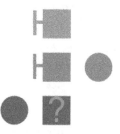

If we look closely, we see that the circles were left behind. This is because, as you may recall from a few pages back, circles (and ellipses) use cx and cy for their center coordinates, not x and y.

I have a better idea:

```
all_groups.attr("transform", "T150,0");
```

Try this out and you'll see that everything fits perfectly. As we get into more complex shapes, we'll see that transformations are the only feasible solution for moving objects around in an efficient manner.

Case Study: Let's Make a Braille Generator

For all its splendid virtues, JavaScript can be a difficult language to teach or learn. While it's capable of orchestrating every nook and cranny of a web page, one needs a fairly sophisticated sense of HTML and the Document Object Model to really understand why the browser needs a scripting language. If you've only just learned how to add an image to a page, your first priority is probably not to start manipulating it with code.

One of the reasons I love Raphael is that it offers a perfect point of entry for new programmers. Rather than get their hands dirty with form validation, DOM selectors, and other bone-dry topics, greenhorn coders can immediately see the fruits of their labor in the form of dots and squares on the page.

If you are one of the uninitiated, the extended example in this interlude will toss you into the fray. If you know JavaScript, it will serve as a tidy example of how to make Raphael work for you: we're going to make a braille generator (see the following reference for the braille alphabet from the Braille Authority of North America (*http://www.brailleauthority.org/*).

ALPHABET AND NUMBERS

1	2	3	4	5	6	7	8	9	0
a	b	c	d	e	f	g	h	i	j

k	l	m	n	o	p	q	r	s	t

u	v	w	x	y	z

The Data

In the example at the end of Chapter 1, we got a taste of using data to generate the specs of the ellipses and circles. We're going to extend that concept here by generating the braille patterns for each character dynamically. (I don't know about you, but I do not feel like manually keying in the definitions for each letter and number by hand.)

Wikipedia comes to our rescue here with a handy chart (*http://bit.ly/braille-ascii*) defining each character as a series of numbers, one through six, indicating which of the spaces in the 3 by 2 matrix should be raised. A quick glance at the chart indicates that the pattern goes like this:

1 4

2 5

3 6

So *V* in braille, which looks like a capital *L* in the Latin alphabet, is 1-2-3-6.

Curiously, this definition takes up more memory than is necessary, since—as many have noted—braille was among the first binary definitions of language. A *V* is really 111001, which takes up more space on the screen but considerably fewer bits. We'll stick with the way Wikipedia has it for simplicity.

I took the liberty of converting the text from the Wikipedia chart into a nice JavaScript object using a little trick called copy-and-paste plus tedious formating by hand.

```
var braille = {
    "A": "1",
    "B": "1-2",
    "C": "1-4",
    "D": "1-4-5",
    "E": "1-5",
    "F": "1-2-4",
```

```
    "G": "1-2-4-5",
    "H": "1-2-5",
    "I": "2-4",
    "J": "2-4-5",
    "K": "1-3",
    "L": "1-2-3",
    "M": "1-3-4",
    "N": "1-3-4-5",
    "O": "1-3-5",
    "P": "1-2-3-4",
    "Q": "1-2-3-4-5",
    "R": "1-2-3-5",
    "S": "2-3-4",
    "T": "2-3-4-5",
    "U": "1-3-6",
    "V": "1-2-3-6",
    "W": "2-4-5-6",
    "X": "1-3-4-6",
    "Y": "1-3-4-5-6",
    "Z": "1-3-5-6"
};
```

From here on out, the longer coding examples will be broken into pieces to prevent us from getting lost in pages and pages of code. If you're following along, you'll see that future functions in this example will refer back to the braille object defined above without re-printing it every time.

Now for the fun part.

The Fun Part

At its core, this app will be drawing dots based on numbers. So let's make a function to take a number from one to six and return a dot in the correct location. For now, we won't worry about where on the screen each collection of dots (or "cell") should go.

```
var paper = Raphael(0, 0, 500, 500),
    SPACING = 14,
    RADIUS = 2;

function make_dot(number) {
    number -= 1; // normalize to 0-5
    if (number < 0 || number > 5) {
        console.log("Invalid number.");
        return null;
    }
    // first or second column
    var x = Math.floor(number / 3);
    // first, second, or third row of that column
```

```
        var y = number % 3;
            var dot = paper.circle(x * SPACING, y * SPACING, RADIUS).attr("fill",
    "black");
        return dot;
    }
```

Hopefully, the comments explain everything you need to know, but you can try it out with make_dot(3) or make_dot(5) to see how it works. We're simply mapping digits to spots in a braille letter's grid. I've defined the spacing and radius of the dots in external variables, capitalized by convention to represent constant values, for easy adjustment if I decide to change the specs later.

Notice that I'm not only creating the dot corresponding to the number, I'm also returning it. This is so that we can collect all of a cell's dots into one Raphael set. If you don't know what a set is, you clearly did not read the previous chapter.

Let's do future generations a favor and allow the function to accept either a string or an array of numbers:

```
function make_cell(dots) {
    // if we get a string, make it an array
    if (typeof dots === "string") {
        dots = dots.split("-");
    }
    var cell = paper.set();

    for (var c = 0; c < dots.length; c += 1) {
        cell.push(make_dot(dots[c]));
    }
    return cell;
}
```

Let's try out a few letters from the chart.

```
paper.text(10, 25, "V:");
make_cell("1-2-3-6").transform("T30,10");

paper.text(10, 85, "J:");
make_cell([2,4,5]).transform("T30,70");
```

We're taking advantage of the fact that JavaScript does not make rigid distinctions about variable type. If we were writing in Python or Java, the compiler would flunk us for splitting a string into smaller strings and then treating them as as numbers just because they happen to be made of digits. JavaScript is a "loosely typed" language, which is computer science speak for "chill."

(Note that you don't actually have to feed the numbers in order here, per my previous comment about using Wikipedia for simplicity.)

Once again, we create and return the Raphael object. Next—almost done here—let's write a function to make an individual word at a specific location on the page. We'll feed

that location as an object with x and y properties, defaulting to {x: 10, y: 10} if no
position is supplied.

```
function make_word(word, pos) {
    pos = pos || { x: 10, y: 10};
    // capitalize
    word = word.toUpperCase();
    var myword = paper.set();
    for (var c = 0; c < word.length; c += 1) {
        // recall that "braille" is the object for the letter definitions
        if (braille[word[c]]) {
            var letter = make_cell(braille[word[c]]);
            myword.push(letter);
            letter.transform("T" + pos.x + "," + pos.y);
            // move over 3 spaces -- two for the width of the letter and
            // a space between
            pos.x += SPACING * 3;
        }
    }
    return myword;
}
```

Give it a shot with something like make_word("Raphael", { x: 10, y: 10 }); and
see the fruit of our labors:

Lastly, we need a function to string words together. We'll try to be smart about it when
it's time to skip to a new line.

```
function make_words(message) {
    var pos = { x: 10, y: 10 },
        words = message.toUpperCase().split(" "),
        myset = paper.set();

    for (var c = 0; c < words.length; c += 1) {
        // see if it's time for a carriage return
        myset.push(make_word(words[c], pos));
            if (pos.x > 10 && (pos.x + SPACING * 3 * words[c].length) > pa-
per.width) {
            pos.x = 10;
            pos.y += SPACING * 5;
        } else {
            pos.x += SPACING * 3;
        }
    }
    return myset;
}
```

See this code live on jsFiddle (*http://jsfiddle.net/raphaeljs/jt3fm/*).

As you can see, Raphael sets nest quite nicely, just like objects (since that's what they are). At each stage—letter, word, phrase—the function returns a Raphael set that is incorporated into a set at the next level. At the highest level, this returns one set with references to every dot on the screen (grouped into sets for letters and words), which allows us to easily erase the canvas and start over.

In the real world, we would probably want to allow users to type something in and see it in braille. No problem:

```
<input id="message" style="width: 200px" value="Raphael is great"/>
<input id="clickme" type="button" value="braille-ify" />
<div id="canvas"></div>

<script>

/* include all of the above code */

var braille_words = paper.set();

function make() {
    // clear any existing words
    braille_words.remove();
    // write new ones, overwriting previous value of set
    braille_words = make_words(document.getElementById("message").value);
};

// click event to invoke function
document.getElementById("clickme").onclick = make;

// call when page loads, which will draw defaul value ("Raphael is great")
make();
</script>
```

See this code live on jsFiddle (*http://jsfiddle.net/raphaeljs/YtLN4/*).

Reflections

Like most problems in programming, Raphael powered apps work by breaking the task into small, manageable routines that can be strung together for more complex behavior. Because it is so neatly modularized, you could easily expand this code to allow for different styles and standards of braille, or pretty much any other visual way to represent alphabets. (I once wrote an app (*http://yhoo.it/signature-app*), overnight, in which a user could type in his or her name and see how it would look as signed by a certain U.S. White House administrator with a comically childish signature. Same concept.)

Since Raphael is just a fancy abstraction of JavaScript, it works perfectly with standard UI components like buttons and input boxes, as you see in the last part of this example. In the next chapter, we'll learn how to orchestrate every aspect of user input to directly manipulate Raphael objects on the screen.

Final Thoughts: Seeing Things

Merely creating an object in JavaScript and calling it a circle does not make this circle appear on the page. All things on a web page, from paragraphs to text to shapes, are represented on the page as *nodes* or *elements*, typically as text surrounded by tags. You probably recognize `<p>This guy</p>` as a paragraph node and `<img src="my dog.png" />` as an image node.

If you right click on the webpage we just made and select "view source," you will not see any evidence of our circle in the HTML. This is not surprising. Raphael draws objects dynamically when the user loads the page, so we would not expect to see the circle hard-coded into the text file that the browser loads from the server. Fortunately, most browsers also allow you to view the source of the live version of the page. Firefox has a great plug-in called Firebug for just this sort of thing, while Chrome and Internet Explorer have a window called "developer tools" included.

In most browsers, you can right-click the element on the page and select "inspect element" to jump right to the live view. Otherwise, make your way to the "HTML" or "elements" tab in one of these tools and you'll see that a new object has appeared. In any modern browser, it will look like this:

```
<circle cx="50" cy="50" r="20" fill="#ff0000" stroke="#0000ff" style=""
stroke-width="3"/>
```

As you see, all of the attributes we assigned to our circle are present as attributes in the element. So what's that `dot` variable we made? That's a JavaScript object that *points* to the "physical" object on the page. You can think of it like the HTML object's shadow in the land of JavaScript.

A JavaScript object never forgets the physical element it represents. To make the connection explicitly, you merely have to append `.node` to the variable, like so:

```
var rec = paper.rect(200, 20, 40, 40);
console.log(rec.node);
```

Run that code and, depending on the browser, you'll see something like this:

```
<rect x="200" y="20" width="40" height="40" r="0" rx="0" ry="0"
    fill="none" stroke="#000"
    style="-webkit-tap-highlight-color: rgba(0, 0, 0, 0);"></rect>
```

What you're seeing is the actual representation of the square on the page, as an SVG element. Adding the `.node` gets you from the *abstraction* of the element to the element itself. If you're dealing with pure Raphael, you may not find yourself needing this feature all that often. But if you want to weave Raphael in with another JavaScript library, then the elements on the page will be the common language you use across all functions.

Of course, not all objects need a shadow. We could just have easily declared the circle without assigning the output to a variable:

```
paper.circle(50, 50, 20);
```

That's all well and good, but what happens when we want to update that object with a color and a wider border down the line? We'd have to dig through the page to find it again—a huge pain—or make sure we assign the object every attribute it needs at the time of its birth—a poor solution for any drawing that aspires to be interactive.

Storing references to our elements in JavaScript opens up a world of possibilities, and it's this relationship that sits at the core of Raphael.

CHAPTER 3

Interaction

Chances are good that you aspire to create something beyond the kindergarten-level shapes we covered in the previous chapter. Don't worry—Raphael handles complex shapes just fine (that was originally the subject of this chapter). But I wanted to skip straight to the interactive aspect of Raphael because it's what makes the library so incredibly powerful. You can make as beautiful an image in Photoshop as you like, but you need Raphael to make it dance on demand.

You may recall that, at the end of the braille example in the previous chapter, we created an input box and a button to trigger the function that drew the dots. It looked like this:

```
<input id="message" style="width: 200px" value="Raphael is great"/>
<input id="clickme" type="button" value="braille-ify" />

<script>
    function make() {
        // make the braille
    };

    // click event to invoke function
    document.getElementById("clickme").onclick = make;
</script>
```

This is the most basic method for creating interactions in JavaScript. It consists of three parts: First is the *event*—in this case, a click of the mouse. Second is the *object* on the page we want to update when the event occurs, which in this case is the button. Last is the *function* that should fire when the even occurs in the context of the specified element. In this case, that function is make.

When we want to control our Raphael objects from the page using regular old HTML objects—buttons, dropdown menus, check boxes, radio buttons—then this is how we do it: by assigning (or "registering") a given event to a certain object and pairing them with a function that manipulates our Raphael objects however we like. In the above example, that function read the contents of the input box and translated it into braille. This is extremely convenient for any sort of visualization or graphic where users are invited to slide bars or click buttons to manipulate the number of Raphael objects or their positions.

In many cases, however, we want to allow the user to interact with Raphael objects themselves, clicking shapes, mousing over paths, and so forth. In Chapter 2, we briefly touched on the .node property that transforms a Raphael object into its "physical" counterpart on the page—from shadow to body. Using the node property, one could theoretically register events on it the same way we controlled the button click above.

But that would be a pain, and this book takes a strong stance against sadism. Fortunately, Raphael comes with in-house methods for handling interactions that make life much easier. If you're familiar with jQuery or any other JavaScript helper library, then events in Raphael will look familiar. If not, they'll look familiar soon.

Raphael Events: The Basics

Let's make a red square, and then attach an event to make it turn blue when we click it:

```
var paper = Raphael(0, 0, 500, 500);

var mysquare = paper.rect(25, 25, 250, 250).attr("fill", "red");

mysquare.click(function(e) {
    this.attr("fill", "blue");
});
```

As you can see, .click() is a method you attach to a Raphael object that creates an event. The argument passed to .click() is the function to fire when the user clicks on the object.

Now would be a good time to remind ourselves that, unlike many languages, functions in JavaScript are themselves objects, just like integers, arrays, and strings. Like those other types of variables, you can declare them and then pass them to other functions. You could equally accomplish the above example like this:

```
var paper = Raphael(0, 0, 500, 500);

var mysquare = paper.rect(25, 25, 250, 250).attr("fill", "red");

function turnMeBlue(e) {
    this.attr("fill", "blue");
}

mysquare.click(turnMeBlue);
```

See this code live on jsFiddle (*http://jsfiddle.net/raphaeljs/mpXah/*).

I prefer the former method, which uses an "anonymous" function, because it's one fewer variable to deal with. But you'll occassionally want to declare a function independently and attach it to several different events. It's mostly a stylistic choice.

To make the event a mouseover instead of a click, just use the `.mouseover()` method:

```
var paper = Raphael(0, 0, 500, 500);

var mysquare = paper.rect(25, 25, 250, 250).attr("fill", "red");

mysquare.mouseover(function(e) {
    this.attr("fill", "blue");
});
```

In terms of user experience, I find this program wanting. Let's at least restore the square to its original red color when the user's mouse leaves its premises.

```
var paper = Raphael(0, 0, 500, 500);

var mysquare = paper.rect(25, 25, 250, 250).attr("fill", "red");

mysquare.mouseover(function(e) {
    this.attr("fill", "blue");
});

mysquare.mouseout(function(e) {
    this.attr("fill", "red");
});
```

You can "chain" events to save a few keystrokes:

```
var paper = Raphael(0, 0, 500, 500);

var mysquare = paper.rect(25, 25, 250, 250).attr("fill", "red");

mysquare.mouseover(function(e) {
    this.attr("fill", "blue");
}).mouseout(function(e) {
    this.attr("fill", "red");
});
```

Removing Events

There may come a time when you want to disable an event handler when the page reaches some state. Each event method has a corresponding method to undo it: `unclick()` for `click()`, `unmouseout()` for `mouseout()`, and so forth.

The *un* functions take as an argument the function assigned to the original event, so you don't want to use anonymous functions for events you'll need to undo later. The following example disables the square's mouseover functionality when the user clicks on it:

```
var paper = Raphael(0, 0, 500, 500);

var mysquare = paper.rect(25, 25, 250, 250).attr("fill", "red");

var mover = function() {
    this.attr("fill", "blue");
}

var mout = function() {
    this.attr("fill", "red");
}

mysquare.mouseover(mover).mouseout(mout).click(function(e) {
    this.attr("fill", "green");
    this.unmouseover(mover);
    this.unmouseout(mout);
});
```

I don't find too many occasions where I need to remove events altogether. What's more likely is that you will want to disable them only under certain circumstances, such as when the user has chosen to disable them. You can effectively disable an event handler without removing it by returning the value false, like so:

```
<input id="on_off" type="button" value="Hover ON" />
<div id="canvas"><div>

<script>
var hover_enabled = true;

function toggleHover() {
    if (hover_enabled) {
        this.value = "Hover OFF";
        hover_enabled = false;
    } else {
        this.value = "Hover ON";
        hover_enabled = true;
    }
}

document.getElementById("on_off").onclick = toggleHover();

var paper = Raphael("canvas", 500, 500);

var mysquare = paper.rect(25, 25, 250, 250).attr("fill", "red");

var mover = function() {
    if (!hover_enabled) {
        return false;
    }
    this.attr("fill", "blue");
}
```

```
var mout = function() {
    if (!hover_enabled) {
        return false;
    }
    this.attr("fill", "red");
}

</script>
```

Events and Sets

Like attributes, events can be applied to sets of objects:

```
var paper = new Raphael(0, 0, 500, 500);

var square = paper.rect(200, 10, 50, 70).attr("fill", "steelblue");
var circle = paper.circle(120, 110, 25).attr("fill", "yellow");
var ellipse = paper.ellipse(60, 150, 30, 15).attr("fill", "orange");

var stuff = paper.set();
stuff.push(square, circle, ellipse);

var label = paper.text(10, 10, "Mouse over an object").attr("text-anchor",
"start");

stuff.mouseover(function(e) {
    label.attr("text", this.attr("fill"));
}).mouseout(function(e) {
    label.attr("text", "Mouse over an object");
});
```

See this code live on jsFiddle (*http://jsfiddle.net/raphaeljs/uhuqR/*).

When you mouse over a shape here, the text object we made in the upper-left corner
updates to list the color of whichever one we just clicked. This is an important point:
the this inside the function refers not the set of objects, but to whichever individual
one you clicked on. This is because sets in Raphael are "psuedo objects"—phantasmal
JavaScript objects that bind elements but have no counterpart on the page.

The .mouseover() and .mouseout() events are extremely useful for creating *"tooltips"*
—boxes that pop up when you mouse over an object that offer some information about
that object. In the example above, we essentially did this with a simple text tooltip that
remains in the upper-left corner.

To make the text follow the mouse, we need to glean the coordinates of the cursor at
the moment it enters the shapes and each moment while it's moving around over the
shape. You may notice that there's a variable e that gets passed to the anonymous function inside the mouseover event. Every event has a variable like this that contains information about the event, like where the mouse is on the screen when it's fired and

what object the user interacted with to trigger the event. We don't actually use e in the previous example, but I always include it out of habit since it's so useful.

 Note that this variable does not automatically exist; you have to pass it to the anonymous function. You can call this variable whatever you like. Most people use e or evt or something similar to remind themselves that it contains information about the event.

The event variable has, among many properties, two called .clientX and .clientY that indicate the coordinates of the mouse at the precise moment when the event fired.

To make this label a tooltip, we merely have to update its x and y coordinates according to the mouse position:

```
stuff.mouseover(function(e) {
    label.attr({
        text: this.attr("fill")),
        x: e.clientX,
        y: e.clientY
    });
});
```

This is a nice upgrade to the user experience, but we're not quite there. While a user's mouse is inside a shape, the label just hangs out at the exact point where the cursor entered the shape's domain. To improve the experience, let's attach the movement of the tooltip to the mousemove() event, which will fire every time the mouse moves while inside the element to which the event is attached. We'll also return the label to its original position in the corner when the mouse leaves the shape.

```
stuff.mouseover(function(e) {
    label.attr("text", this.attr("fill"));
}).mousemove(function(e) {
    label.attr({
        x: e.clientX + 10,
        y: e.clientY
    });
}).mouseout(function(e) {
    label.attr({
        x: 10,
        y: 10,
        text: "Mouse over an object"
    });
});
```

You may notice I made one other small improvement: I'm placing the tooltip 10 pixels to the right of the mouse position. This is because, otherwise, it's very easy for the mouse to "trip" over the tooltip itself, prematurely triggering the mouseout event since the cursor is technically leaving the domain of the shape to enter the domain of the tooltip itself. This is useful to remember: the mouse events we attach to a shape do not apply whenever the mouse is inside the bounds of that shape, but rather when the mouse is directly interacting with the shape.

In addition to .click(), .mouseover(), and .mouseout(), Raphael offers the following events: .mousedown(), .mouseup(), .mousemove(), .dblclick(), and .drag(). That last one is a little more complicated, but the others work the same way as a .click(). Let's look at another example.

Drag Events

You could technically make click and drag behavior only with the mouseup, mouse down, and mousemove events, using variables outside the scope of the event handler functions to track when the mouse was pressed on an object and when it was released. In that sense, the drag event is really just a "convenience method" to avoid all that repetitive coding. (You might argue that all of Raphael is really just one large convenience method for the pain of manipulating DOM events. For more discussion of the deep philosophical underpinnings of Raphael, you'll have to wait for the sequel to this book.)

The drag function takes three arguments, all functions: the handlers for the start of the drag, the movement of the mouse during the drag, and the end of the drag:

```
var paper = new Raphael(0, 0, 500, 500);

var circle = paper.circle(120, 110, 25).attr("fill", "yellow");

circle.drag(dragstart, dragmove, dragend);
```

If we consult the Raphael documentation for the drag event (*http://bit.ly/element-doc*), we see that these three functions each come with different arguments:

```
function dragstart(x, y, e) {}
function dragmove(dx, dy, x, y, e) {}
function dragend(e) {}
```

For all three functions, the e variable is the same event variable we see in the other types of handlers. Additionally, x and y in the first two functions record the current position of the mouse. In the second function, dx and dy represent the difference in mouse position between x and y and the original position of the mouse.

Like the e argument we discussed above, these are arguments that you are resposible for passing to the handlers, and you can name them whatever you like. Whatever variables you pass to the dragmove function, for example, Raphael will understand the first one to be the dx value, the second to be the dy value, and so forth. There isn't usually much reason to invent a different naming convention.

Here is how we make a draggable circle:

```
var paper = new Raphael(0, 0, 500, 500);
var circle = paper.circle(120, 110, 25).attr("fill", "yellow");

circle.drag(dragmove, dragstart, dragend);

function dragmove(dx, dy, x, y, e) {
    this.attr({
        cx: x,
        cy: y
    });
}

function dragstart(x, y, e) {
    this.attr("fill", "orange");
}

function dragend(e) {
    this.attr("fill", "yellow");
}
```

See this code live on jsFiddle (*http://jsfiddle.net/raphaeljs/923Pa/*).

We're using the dragstart and dragend functions here to turn the circle orange while it's being dragged and to return it to its yellow color when the mouse is released. Meanwhile, dragmove is firing several times a second so long as the mouse is moving, resetting the center position to the position of the mouse so that the circle drags along with the mouse.

Observant readers will notice that dragmove comes *before* dragstart in the order of functions that .drag() accepts, which seems to violate common sense. The reason is that the event handler for mouse movements is the only one we absolutely need to make a drag work. In fact, in the above example, the only thing the start and stop functions are accomplishing is changing the color. We'll see in just a moment how we can put them to better use.

Better Dragging

The above example is a good start, but there are a few things I don't like about it. First, it behaves a little differently depending on where in the circle you initially click, since it resets the center of the shape to that point whether you click the very edge or the precise center. The code is also only useful for circles and ellipses, which have cx and cy properties. Attempting to apply this code to a rectangle would be useless.

Instead, let's use the transform() method we learned in the previous chapter. There are a few different ways we could do this. I'm going to skip straight to the best one:

```
var paper = new Raphael(0, 0, 500, 500);
var circle = paper.circle(120, 110, 25).attr("fill", "yellow");

circle.drag(dragmove, dragstart, dragend);

function dragstart(x, y, e) {
    // save the value of the transformation at the start of the drag
    // if this is the initial drag, it will be a blank string
    this.current_transform = this.transform();
    // just for kicks
    this.attr("fill", "orange");
}

function dragmove(dx, dy, x, y, e) {
    // adjust the pre-existing transformation (if any) by the drag difference
    this.transform(this.current_transform+'T'+dx+','+dy);
}

function dragend(e) {
    // update the current transformation with the final value
    this.current_transform = this.transform();
    // that's enough kicks
    this.attr("fill", "yellow");
}
```

Transformations, we should recall, overwrite any previous transformations on the element. Consider the following code:

```
var paper = Raphael(0, 0, 500, 500);

paper.ellipse(300, 200, 50, 20)
    .attr("fill", "green")
    .transform("T5000,1000")
    .transform("T50,10");
```

This does not place the center of the ellipse at (5350,1210). It places it at (100,30), since the second transformation overwrites the first (absurd) one. In this sense, transformations operate like CSS: applying two colors to an element doesn't mix them, it uses the second one.

If we only used the dragmove function, the drag would only work once. Dragging it a second time would reset the position to the original one. By dutifully recording the last known position at the end of each drag and adding it to the next one, we get a fully mobile object. Not only is it responsive to where on the object we click, this precise strategy works for any shape—circles, squares, and more complex shapes that we'll learn about in the next chapter. Better yet, it works on all of those types at once when those shapes are bundled in a set.

Dragging Sets

If you check out the Raphael section of a coding forum like Stack Overflow—what else is there to do on a Saturday night?—one of the most common questions you will see is how to make sets of objects draggable. This comes up all the time with browser games and complex user interfaces.

People come up with all sorts of hilariously intricate solutions that involve iterating though each item in the list, calculating where it needs to be, and individually moving it. I'm here to tell you that there is a better way.

First, let's make one improvement to the above example. Right now, we're assigning the transformation as a property of the object this, the same way we might give any object in JavaScript a property. In general, I don't think it's a great idea to be adding properties to objects you didn't create from scratch—particularly ones with lots of awesome properties like Raphael objects—since there is always the chance that you will overwrite some pre-existing property or method. Of more direct relevance to us is that assigning a property to a set in Raphael does not transfer that property to each constituent item. That only works when performing a standard Raphael operation. Fortunately, Raphael has precisely the function we need: .data().

The .data() method stores arbitrary values in keys, very similar to the way information is stored in regular JS objects, but with a slightly more burdensome syntax.

```
// old way
this.current_transform = this.transform();
console.log(this.current_transform);

// better way
this.data("current_transform") = this.transform();
console.log(this.data("current_transform"));
```

Like .attr(), .transform(), and most other Raphael methods, leaving out the second argument turns .data() from an assignment to a retrieval. With that in mind, let's make a draggable set of heterogeneous objects—say, a face from a six-sided die.

```
var paper = Raphael(0, 0, 500, 500);

var dice = paper.set();

// rectangle with rounded edges
dice.push(paper.rect(10, 10, 60, 60, 4).attr("fill", "#FFF"));

dice.push(paper.circle(22, 58, 5).attr("fill", "#000"));
dice.push(paper.circle(58, 22, 5).attr("fill", "#000"));
dice.push(paper.circle(40, 40, 5).attr("fill", "#000"));
dice.push(paper.circle(22, 22, 5).attr("fill", "#000"));
dice.push(paper.circle(58, 59, 5).attr("fill", "#000"));
```

The construction of the die is pretty straightforward save for one small new concept. A `.rect()` object can take a fifth argument that rounds the corners with a radius of the given number of pixels. Note that we have a white background to the die face as well. It doesn't make any visual difference so long as the page itself is white, but it makes a huge behavioral difference. Without a filling, Raphael considers the object to be empty, and thus clicking inside it has no effect. The dragging event would not work because there there would not be anything for the mouse to hold on to.

We're going to be attaching the drag events to this set. But as I so presciently pointed out earlier, an event attached to a set still fires only on the specific element that the user clicks. We need to make sure that the drag functionality applies to every piece of the set simultaneously.

At this point, you may be thinking, "Easy, I'll just perform the transformation on the variable dice from inside the event function." Sure, that would work—so long as there is there is only ever one die on the page. I don't know what sort of lame games you like to play, but the ones I play have two. Do you really want to keep track of a different variable for each die?

No, you don't. You want some way for the children of a set to locate their parent. For that, we'll use the `.data()` method to give the items a property called myset.

```
// pair the objects in the set to the set itself
dice.data("myset", dice);
```

Then it's a matter of locating the child element's parent and operating on it. Transformations are always relative to an object's original position, so the transformation will be identical on each item. Because of that, we can use the transformation of any object and apply it to the whole group.

```
dice.drag(
    function(dx, dy, x, y, e) {
        //dragmove
        var myset = this.data("myset");
        myset.transform(this.data("mytransform")+'T'+dx+','+dy);
    },
    function(x, y, e) {
        //dragstart
        var myset = this.data("myset");
        myset.data("mytransform", this.transform());
    },
    function(e) {
        //dragend
        var myset = this.data("myset");
        myset.data("mytransform", this.transform());
    }
);
```

See this code live on jsFiddle (*http://jsfiddle.net/raphaeljs/LQ4kw/*).

I used three anonymous functions there for the sake of variety, but we could actually save a few lines by declaring the functions separately, since the start and end functions are identical. Now let's get creative!

Case Study: Let's Play Dominoes

I always thought the purpose of dominoes was to line them up on their sides and knock them over, particularly if it was your little sister who set them up. But apparently it's also a nonviolent game. Let's make a set. (I like this example because we can reuse a lot of the same code from the braille section.)

Wikipedia tells us that "the traditional set of dominoes contains one unique piece for each possible combination of two ends with zero to six spots." Let's begin by repurposing the function that constructs a letter of braille to make a die face, which requires nine positions instead of six:

```
1 4 7
2 5 8
3 6 9
```

I find it easier to just write out the patterns than to write a function to generate them, but feel free to do it the hard way on your own time. Like the braille example, RADIUS will refer to the size of the dots and SPACING will refer to the space between them. Thus, each half of a piece will have a width of 3 * SPACING.

```
var paper = Raphael(0,0,900,900),
    SPACING = 18,
    RADIUS = 4;

var patterns = [
    "",           // 0 dots
    "5",          // 1 dot
    "3-7",        // 2 dots
    "3-5-7",      // 3 dots
    "1-3-7-9",    // 4 dots
    "1-3-5-7-9",  // 5 dots
    "1-2-3-7-8-9" // 6 dots
];
```

We'll use nearly the exact same functions for the pips and individual squares, merely adding a square outline and adjusting the spacing a bit. We'll be calling the make_face() function twice for each individual domino tile.

```
function make_dot(number) {
    number -= 1;
    if (number < 0 || number > 9) {
        console.log("Invalid number.");
        return null;
```

```
    }
    // first, second, or third column
    var x = Math.floor(number / 3);
    // first, second, or third row of that column
    var y = number % 3;
     var dot = paper.circle(x * SPACING + SPACING / 2, y * SPACING + SPACING /
2, RADIUS).attr("fill", "black");
    return dot;
}

function make_face(dots) {
    if (typeof dots === "string") {
        dots = dots.split("-");
    }
    var tile = paper.set();

    //square
    tile.push(paper.rect(0, 0, SPACING * 3, SPACING * 3).attr({ fill: "#FFF"}));

    //dots
    for (var c = 0; c < dots.length; c += 1) {
        tile.push(make_dot(dots[c]));
    }

    return tile;
}
```

The next part will be a little fancier. Instead of using the `.data()` property, we're going to store all the information we need about each tile in a closure—variables that live inside a function that returns an object. Objects in closures are protected like private properties of a class in languages like Java or C. For a thorough discussion of closures, refer to Chapter Four of your copy of *JavaScript: The Good Parts*.

The end result will be to create an object with functions to move and rotate the tiles. Here's the first part:

```
function tile(num_dots_top, num_dots_bottom, x, y, a) {
    if (typeof(num_dots_top) === "undefined" || typeof(num_dots_top) ===
    "undefined") {
        console.log("You must supply values for both sides of the tile.");
        return null;
    }

    // positional info. Defaults
    var pos = { x: x || 0, y: y || 0, a: a || 0 },
        centroid = { x: pos.x + SPACING * 1.5, y: pos.y + SPACING * 3 };

    // Raphael objects
    var top = make_face(patterns[num_dots_top]),
        bottom = make_face(patterns[num_dots_bottom]),
        piece = paper.set([top, bottom]);
```

```
    // function to place piece at x,y location, rotated to angle a (in degrees)
    var move = function(x, y, a) {
        pos = {x: x, y: y, a: a};
        centroid = { x: pos.x + SPACING * 1.5, y: pos.y + SPACING * 3 };
        top.transform("T" + x + "," + y + "R" + a + "," + centroid.x + "," +
centroid.y);
        y += SPACING * 3;
        bottom.transform("T" + x + "," + y + "R" + a + "," + centroid.x + "," +
centroid.y);
    };

    // initial position
    move(pos.x, pos.y, pos.a);
```

The (as yet incomplete) tile() function will be called once each time we need a new tile. The tiles' coordinates and its rotation are stored in the pos object. This function will make internal use of the nested move() function to get the piece where we want it and rotate it to the desired angle using both the T and R transformations.

Each time the move function is called, we update the pos variable and recalculate the coordinates of the center of the tile, which we will need for the axis of rotation. Then the function moves the top half of the piece. We'll deal with compound transformations in more detail later, but this one is pretty straightforward. First, we move the top square to the given x and y coordinates, then we rotate it around the center point that we just calculated.

Since the bottom tile needs to appear under the top one, let's add 3 * SPACING to the y value before running the same transformation; we update y instead of pos.y so as not to modify the stored position of the tile.

Now let's add a drag capability. We want to be able to use the move() variable to drag objects as well, but there's a small hitch: The function updates the position of the tile each time it executes, but the dx and dy variables represent the total amount of distance the mouse has moved since the drag began. If we were to update the position of the tile with each call of dragmove, the tile would very quickly fly off the screen.

Easily solved: we just need the function to remember where it was when the drag began.

```
    // drag variables
    var dragx, dragy;

    // drag handlers
    var dragstart = function(x, y, e) {
        dragx = pos.x;
        dragy = pos.y;
    };

    var dragmove = function(dx, dy, x, y, e) {
        move(dragx + dx, dragy + dy, angle);
    };
```

```
    piece.drag(dragmove, dragstart);

    // rotation
    piece.dblclick(function(e) {
        angle += 90;
        move(pos.x, pos.y, angle);
    });
```

There's no need for a `dragend` function here since the position is updated each time.

The final event handler this function needs is a double click for rotating the piece, and it needs to return something so that all the hard work isn't lost. I suggest returning the `move()` function itself in case we need to call it manually after it has returned.

```
    return {
        move: move
    };
} // close the function
```

Here it is altogether:

```
function tile(num_dots_top, num_dots_bottom, x, y, a) {
    if (typeof(num_dots_top) === "undefined" || typeof(num_dots_top) ===
    "undefined") {
        console.log("You must supply values for both sides of the tile.");
        return null;
    }

    // positional info. Defaults
    var pos = { x: x || 0, y: y || 0, a: a || 0 },
        centroid = { x: pos.x + SPACING * 1.5, y: pos.y + SPACING * 3 };

    // Raphael objects
    var top = make_face(patterns[num_dots_top]),
        bottom = make_face(patterns[num_dots_bottom]),
        piece = paper.set([top, bottom]);

    // function to place piece at x,y location, rotated to angle a (in degrees)
    var move = function(x, y, a) {
        pos = {x: x, y: y, a: a};
        centroid = { x: pos.x + SPACING * 1.5, y: pos.y + SPACING * 3 };
        top.transform("T" + x + "," + y + "R" + a + "," + centroid.x + "," +
centroid.y);
        y += SPACING * 3;
        bottom.transform("T" + x + "," + y + "R" + a + "," + centroid.x + "," +
centroid.y);
    };

    // initial position
    move(pos.x, pos.y, pos.a);

    // drag variables
```

```
var dragx, dragy;

// drag handlers
var dragstart = function(x, y, e) {
    dragx = pos.x;
    dragy = pos.y;
};

var dragmove = function(dx, dy, x, y, e) {
    move(dragx + dx, dragy + dy, angle);
};

piece.drag(dragmove, dragstart);

// rotation
piece.dblclick(function(e) {
    angle += 90;
    move(pos.x, pos.y, angle);
});

return {
    move: move
};
} // close the function
```

For an actual game, one would presumably want to randomly generate a certain number of tiles. For testing, let's make a complete set of tiles. To do so, just call the function for every unique combination of numbers using a nested loop. We'll save references to the tiles in an object. Since there are 28 tiles, four rows of seven seems logical.

```
var tiles = {};
var count = 0;

for (var c = 0; c <= 6; c += 1) {
    for (var i = c; i <= 6; i += 1) {
        var t = tile(c, i, 10 + (SPACING * 3 + 10) * (count % 7), 10 + (SPACING
* 6 + 10) * Math.floor(count / 7));
        tiles[c + "-" + i] = t;
        count += 1;
    }
}
```

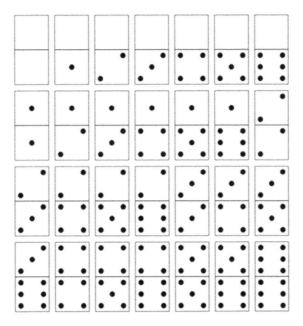

See this code live on jsFiddle (*http://jsfiddle.net/raphaeljs/Sq9vt/*).

Fire this up and you'll see 28 beautiful tiles. You can drag and rotate them to your heart's delight.

There is one small improvement I want to make. When objects overlap, the one that was most recently added to the page gets displayed on top; this is known as *paint order*. When manipulating a particular tile, we would like it to appear above its neighbors. Raphael offers convenient functions called toFront() and toBack() that can move an element or set it above or behind the rest of the elements on the canvas. It's a matter of taste where we want to attach the function. I'm going to stick it on a mouseover() event so that players can browse tiles by grazing the screen, but if this seems too intrusive, mousedown() is a fine alternative.

This can go anywhere in the tile() function after piece is defined:

```
piece.mouseover(function(e) {
    piece.toFront();
});
```

It might also occur to you to simply stick the toFront() call in the move() function. While I like the way you think, I don't love the idea that this method would be called many times a second during a drag. Behind the scenes, Raphael is rearranging the elements in the DOM to get the one you need on top. Let's not ask it to do so unnecessarily often.

There isn't space here to code the rules of the game—also, I don't feel like learning them—but I would submit that doing so would be easy compared to the hard but fruitful work of making the set. You would probably start by adding a `dragend()` event handler to snap a piece to the nearest open position on the board, then check the adjacent pieces to see if the move is valid. Even adding a secret code for "evil big brother" to scatter the tiles is easily within the realm of possibility, though it would be a lot cooler with animations. That sounds like an excellent topic for a future chapter.

Final Thoughts

Event handlers are the ambassadors of the Web, shuffling between your users and your code. Any web page is fundamentally a collection of things that you present to other people: images, boxes of text, menus, buttons, and, if you're reading this, shapes and lines.

Raphael allows you to make those things resemble the actual world with far greater verisimilitude, whether it's dominoes or something larger. (In the next chapter, we're going to make a baseball field.) It is my experience that things in the real world are not all bolted down—I'm fortunate to have avoided prison—and the methods in this chapter allow you to make those things come alive.

CHAPTER 4
Paths: How to Make Custom Shapes and Curves

Circles and squares are great for getting started with Raphael, but eventually you will probably want to branch out into something more complex. For that, we will use paths, a relatively simple set of instructions capable of making almost any shape or drawing you can imagine: squiggly lines, donuts, and figure eights, as well as complex shapes like people or animals.

To understand how paths work, consider the following standby of those tedious workplace team-building workshops: you and a partner have been placed back-to-back with a matching set of colored pencils. You each have a blank sheet of paper. Your job is to draw a picture and give your partner verbal instructions on how to recreate this picture on his or her own sheet of paper. No peeking.

To make things a little easier, let's make it graphing paper.

First, you would be wise to establish with your partner that the upper-leftmost point on the paper has the coordinates (0,0). Then you might go about it something like this:

1. "Using your pink pencil, start on the point at the coordinates (3,4), and draw a straight line eight units to the right."

2. "Go down five units."

3. "From there, draw a diagonal line back to the original point."

4. "Then, using your green pencil, fill in the space bounded by those lines."

Assuming you've been paired with a halfway competent coworker, you should both now have a green triangle with a pink border. (Hopefully you don't work for a design company.)

For the next shape, you would probably say something like "Start a new shape on the coordinates (15,22)" so that your partner doesn't accidentally draw a line from the ending point of the last shape to the new one, Etch A Sketch style.

In case you haven't guessed, your partner here is a computer. Drawing paths in Raphael is an alchemical process of transforming instructions into shapes. And your partner never messes up, so long as you don't.

Syntax

Paths are represented in browsers as a long string of characters. These strings can be broken down into a series of points that tell the computer where to start, where to end up, and what to do on the way there.

A simple path might look like this:

```
var d = "M 10,30 L 60,30 L 10,80 L 60,80";
```

This translates to: "Move (M) to the coordinates (10,30), draw a line (L) to the coordinates (60,30), then a line (L) to (10,80), and then a line (L) to (60,80)."

To see what a path looks like, initialize a Raphael project by declaring a new paper object on a page, and add this line:

```
var paper = Raphael(0,0,300,300);
var d = "M 10,30 L 60,30 L 10,80 L 60,80";
var mark = paper.path(d);
```

As you see, we made a Z pattern starting at (10,30) and ending at (60,80). All we had to do was tell Raphael where to start and define the three points it should visit, tracing a line behind it as it goes.

You have a little wiggle room when it comes to the precise syntax for paths. The spaces between the letters and the numbers aren't necessary, since the browser has no difficulty distinguishing when one segment ends and the next begins. The commas between numbers can be replaced with spaces if you prefer. Your syntax will probably condense as you get more experienced.

Dressing Up Your Paths

Paths can take many of the same attributes as shapes, including stroke (the style governing lines) and fill (governing the space enclosed by those lines). To make a slightly less anemic-looking Z, let's give it a few properties:

```
mark.attr({
    "stroke": "#F00",
    "stroke-width": 3
});
```

See this code live on jsFiddle (*http://jsfiddle.net/raphaeljs/RnBMA/*).

If you're fuzzy on why the browser understands #F00 as the color red, read up on "hexadecimal color codes."

Just to see what happens, let's also add some interior color:

```
mark.attr("fill", "#00C");
```

Hmmm. Since a *Z* is not a "closed" figure, in which the last point rejoins the first, Raphael guesses what to fill in by drawing an imaginary line from the end point to the starting point and then filling in anything that's bounded on all sides by lines. (This is in stark contrast to the old days of Microsoft Paint, when the fill tool would paint the entire screen if there was even a single pixel missing along the perimeter of your shape.) While the computer is reasonably smart about guessing what to do in these circumstances, it's much better to just complete your shapes if you want them to have some internal color.

To do so, you could just add a final L10,30 command to the end of the path string, thus drawing a final line that reconnects with the original. The path syntax also offers a convenient command to do the same thing. If you end your path with a z, it connects to the beginning automatically. Let's try it alongside an alternate syntax for the path, just to make sure I was telling the truth above:

```
var paper = Raphael(0,0,300,300);
var d = "M10 30L60 30L10 80L60 80z";
var mark = paper.path(d);
```

Relative paths

The commands M and L have younger siblings, m and l, which function identically except for one key factor: they understand coordinates to be relative to the previous coordinate. We could achieve the exact same *Z* in a more intuitive manner like this:

```
var d = "M10,30l50,0l-50,50l50,0";
```

We started at the same point—using a lowercase m here would be meaningless since we don't have a starting point to be relative to—and then told the computer to move its imaginary pen 50 pixels to the right and zero pixels up, then to the left 50 and down 50, then 50 to the right again.

For simple cases like this one, it's often much easier to use relative coordinates. In other cases, you'll have predetermined points on the screen that you'll want to connect without doing the math of how far apart they are relative to one another. It's up to you, and you can mix and match capital and lowercase letters in the same string.

There are two more commands that make life a little easier: H, V, and their tagalong siblings h and v, for "horizontal" and "vertical." These commands only expect one number to follow them, and assume the other is zero. We can simplify our Z again like so (I've mixed in a capital and lowercase H for demonstration):

```
var d = "M10,30h50l-50,50H60";
```

Hopping Around

Paths should always begin with an M. But if you need to "pick up the pen" during the course of drawing a path to jump to another spot, you can also use the M or m in the middle of the string. Here's a capital *I*:

```
var I = paper.path("M40,10h30m-15,0v50m-15,0h30");
```

This is another example where the relative coordinates that come using lowercase letters are very convenient. But just for practice, let's make the same *I* using only "absolute" coordinates:

```
var I = paper.path("M40,10H70M55,10V60M40,60H70")
```

Let's say we want to make some solid shapes, like this irregular triangle, beginning from the lower right vertex:

```
var d = "M90,90l-80,-20L50,5L90,90";
var tri = paper.path(d).attr({
    "fill": "yellow",
    "stroke-width": 5
});
```

Since we were careful to make the last point the same as the first, there is no ambiguity as to what should get filled in. Here we have something that looks like a yield sign restructured by a driver who did not, in fact, yield:

Again, we can freely mix uppercase and lowercase letters in a path string, though doing so may not contribute to one's sanity during the creation of complex shapes.

Behind the scenes, Raphael stores paths as an array in which each object represents one command of a letter and some numbers. If you were to add the line console.log(tri) at the end of the previous example and examine your code in Firebug, you would see something like this:

```
[Array[3], Array[3], Array[3], Array[3], toString: function]
    0: Array[3]
        0: "M"
        1: 90
        2: 90
        length: 3
1: Array[3]
0: "L"
1: 10
2: 70
length: 3
2: Array[3]
0: "L"
1: 50
2: 5
length: 3
3: Array[3]
0: "L"
1: 90
2: 90
length: 3
```

The careful reader will note that Raphael converted the second point to absolute coordinates when converting the string to the array.

It's useful to understand how Raphael stores paths for the purpose of debugging and getting information about the path after the fact. (Perhaps you want the coordinates of the first and last point in order to draw some objects at either end of a line.) In fact, you can choose to deliver a path command to Raphael in this format as well. You can get the same irregular triangle in the above example using the array form:

```
var tri = paper.path([["M", 90, 90], ["L", 10, 70], ["L", 50, 5], ["L", 90, 90]]);
```

I personally find it easier and more concise to use the string format and let Raphael deal with converting it to an array, but the choice is yours.

Polygons

Given how common rectangles are in design, it makes sense for Raphael to offer a .rect() function, even if it duplicates what can be done with paths with a few more lines. (Actually, this is a decision baked into the SVG specifications, not a shortcut unique to our library.) It would be highly inefficient, on the other hand, for Raphael to offer a .pentagon(), .hexagon(), and so forth. Fortunately, we now know enough to make any regular polygon we like. Let's write a function to make a polygon of N sides centered around an arbitrary point. It's going to take a very small amount of trigonometry—three lines, I think—but we'll get through it together. The function we're going to write will take the center coordinates (like a circle or ellipse), the number of sides in our regular polygon, and the length of the sides, and return the path as a string.

```
function NGon(x, y, N, side) {
    // draw a dot at the center point for visual reference
    paper.circle(x, y, 3).attr("fill", "black");

    var path = "", n, temp_x, temp_y, angle;

    for (n = 0; n <= N; n += 1) {
        // the angle (in radians) as an nth fraction of the whole circle
        angle = n / N * 2 * Math.PI;

        // The starting x value of the point adjusted by the angle
        temp_x = x + Math.cos(angle) * side;
        // The starting y value of the point adjusted by the angle
        temp_y = y + Math.sin(angle) * side;

        // Start with "M" if it's the first point, otherwise L
        path += (n === 0 ? "M" : "L") + temp_x + "," + temp_y;
    }
    return path;
}
```

Let's fire this baby up with a few different values and see how we did.

```
var paper = Raphael(0, 0, 500, 500);

paper.path(NGon(40, 40, 6, 30));
paper.path(NGon(130, 60, 9, 40));
paper.path(NGon(240, 160, 25, 80));
```

See this code live on jsFiddle (*http://jsfiddle.net/raphaeljs/U9bxc/*).

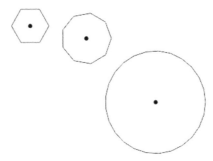

As you see, a 25-sided polygon is pretty close to a circle, as we might expect. You might even say a circle is a polygon with infinite sides. From there, *RaphaelJS* will leave you to your musings.

Curves

Drawing lines that bend and curve is necessarily more difficult in Raphael because you have more decisions to make. So we're drawing a curve from point A to point B. Should it curve up or down? By how much? Is it symmetrical?

The SVG specifications offer a couple of different commands for curves, but the documentation is pretty miserable. In this chapter, we're going to cover the most intuitive type, the ellipitical curve.

The A Command: Elliptical Curves

As you might predict, this command creates curves that look like segments taken from an ellipse. As such, they require a few peices of information. Don't worry if this is confusing at first. It's naturally confusing, but a few examples will illuminate these parameters.

Like lines, elliptical curves begin at the point where the previous command left off.

An A command looks like this: `C 50,75 0 0,1 400,200`. Those numbers represent:

- The horizontal and vertical radii of the imaginary ellipse we're using as a guide
- An angle rotating the curve's axis (for advanced users)
- A Boolean value (or "flag") that is either `0` or `1`, representing whether a curve goes clockwise or counterclockwise
- A Boolean value (or "flag") representing whether the curve goes the long way or the short way
- The ending point

To explore what this means, we're going to start with a point at [50, 50] and end at a point at [200, 125]. Let's draw that and make some dotted lines for reference:

```
var paper = Raphael(0, 0, 500, 4000);
var starting_point = paper.circle(150, 150, 4).attr({ fill: "green", stroke:
0 });
var ending_point = paper.circle(250, 220, 4).attr({ fill: "red", stroke: 0 });

var path1 = paper.path("M 150,150 L 250,150 L 250,220").attr(
"stroke-dasharray", ".");
var path2 = paper.path("M 150,150 v 70 h 100").attr("stroke-dasharray", "-");
```

So far, so good:

Let's try an elliptical arc with the angle and these two mysterious boolean values set to zero. We'll use the length and the height of this rectangle as the radii.

```
var curve1 = paper.path("M150,150 A100,70 0 0,0 250,220")
            .attr({"stroke-width": 2, stroke: "blue"});
```

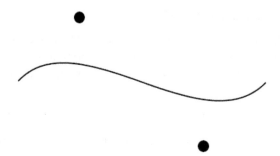

Nice—we have a beautiful sloping curve connecting the points. Let's see what happens when we set the first flag to 1 instead of 0:

```
var curve2 = paper.path("M150,150 A100,70 0 1,0 250,220")
            .attr({"stroke-width": 2, stroke: "cyan"});
```

Whoa. The starting and ending points are the same, and we're still following the path of an ellipse with the same radii, but we went the long way. The SVG specification calls this the "long arc flag," but I like to call it the "detour value." If the detour value is zero or false, the curve takes the shorter path to the destination. If it's one, it takes the longer path.

Let's try the other flag, setting the detour flag back to 0:

```
var curve3 = paper.path("M150,150 A100,70 0 0,1 250,220")
                .attr({"stroke-width": 2, stroke: "pink"});
```

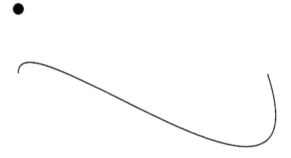

This is the same as the first curve, but it takes a clockwise path instead of counterclockwise path. This is officially known as the "sweep flag," but I like to think of it as the "clockwise flag." You may notice that curve 3 "completes" curve 2, since its flags have opposite values.

Can you guess what our last combination of flags looks like? If you said "a clockwise flag that takes the long way to get to its final destination," you were correct:

```
var curve4 = paper.path("M150,150 A100,70 0 1,1 250,220")
                .attr({"stroke-width": 2, stroke: "orange"});
```

Put together, we see that the four combinations describe the two ways an ellipse with an x radius of 100 and a y radius of 70 can intersect our starting and ending points:

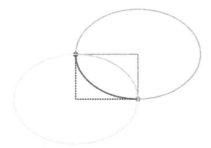

See this code live on jsFiddle (*http://jsfiddle.net/raphaeljs/T8C8p/*).

What about that fifth parameter, the angle, that we've so far been setting to zero? It's a common mistake to assume that this is the angle that the curve traverses, but this is not the case. That angle is calculated automatically based on the radii and the end point—no further information is needed. The angle that you set explicitly will rotate the imaginary ellipses. The easiest way to express this is visually. Let's take the four arcs we just drew and rotate each of them by 45 degrees:

```
var curve1 = paper.path("M150,150 A100,70 45 0,0 250,220")
                .attr({"stroke-width": 2, stroke: "blue"});
var curve2 = paper.path("M150,150 A100,70 45 1,0 250,220")
                .attr({"stroke-width": 2, stroke: "cyan"});
var curve3 = paper.path("M150,150 A100,70 45 0,1 250,220")
                .attr({"stroke-width": 2, stroke: "pink"});
var curve4 = paper.path("M150,150 A100,70 45 1,1 250,220")
                .attr({"stroke-width": 2, stroke: "orange"});
```

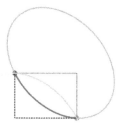

See this code live on jsFiddle (*http://jsfiddle.net/raphaeljs/T8C8p/1/*).

As we can see, we have identically sized ellipses passing through the same points, and then rotated. It's actually a pretty neat geometric property, but I find it difficult to visualize. That said, I confess that I have never once found the need to rotate my elliptical curves in the wild.

The C Command: Cubic Bézier Curves

The elliptical curve is extremely useful in schematics and other geometric drawings. Most of the curves we observe in art and nature, however, do not neatly fit along the path of an ellipse. In these cases, we make use of the cubic Bézier curve.

The C command takes three pairs of coordinates: the destination and two *control points* that determine how the line bends. In most cases, the curve does not pass through these control points. Instead, we can think of them as invisible magnets that pull the line in their direction as it travels to its destination. This is best illustrated with a few examples in which we will place black dots over the control points for educational purposes.

To draw a cubic Bézier curve, one supplies these two control points first and then the destination as the third coordinate. Like all of the other SVG paths, it begins wherever the previous command left off.

```
var paper = Raphael(0,0,500,500);

// draw the control points for educational purposes
var cp1 = paper.circle(100, 50, 4).attr("fill", "black");
var cp2 = paper.circle(200, 150, 4).attr("fill", "black");

// draw the bezier curve
var path = "M 50,100 C 100,50 200,150 250,100";
paper.path(path);
```

See this code live on jsFiddle (*http://jsfiddle.net/raphaeljs/JpNvt/*).

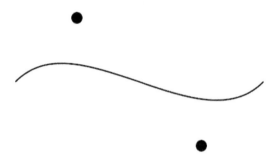

This path begins at coordinates (50,100) and ends up at (250,100), just like a regular old L path. For the first two arguments, I set one control point above the line to the right of the starting point and a second one below and to the left.

If I move the first contol point to be below the starting point as well, at the same x position, the curve assumes a more familiar shape:

```
var paper = Raphael(0,0,500,500);
var cp1 = paper.circle(100, 150, 4).attr("fill", "black");
var cp2 = paper.circle(200, 150, 4).attr("fill", "black");

var path = "M 50,100 C 100,150 200,150 250,100";
paper.path(path);
```

These examples both have some flavor of symmetry, but there's no reason the points need to reflect one another. Here's a wackier example:

```
var paper = Raphael(0,0,500,500);
var path = "M 50,100 C 50,50 300,250 250,100";
var cp1 = paper.circle(50, 50, 4).attr("fill", "black");
```

```
var cp2 = paper.circle(300, 250, 4).attr("fill", "black");
paper.path(path);
```

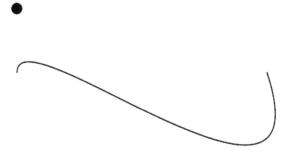

Exotic Paths

The SVG path specifications (*http://bit.ly/path-specs*) contain several more advanced commands for Bézier-like curves that reflect back on themselves. I will freely admit that I've never once found a use for any of them. Should you wish to dive in, an understanding of control points is all you need to get a sense for how they work. You can see a lovely interactive example (*http://jsfiddle.net/raphaeljs/Mfzn8/*) on jsFiddle of one such exotic curve that allows you to manipulate the control points with your mouse.

Case Study: Play Ball!

We have a few other types of curves to cover, but I'd like to point out that, halfway through Chapter 4—and that includes the Introduction, where you didn't even learn anything—we have already accumulated the skills to draw a baseball field.

Looking over Major League Baseball's official rules (*http://atmlb.com/rules-list*), it looks like the minimum allowable distance from home plate to the foul pole is 250 feet. To make our visualization maximally flexible, let's set that value as a variable, along with one for the scale of the graphic and point of origin for home plate:

```
//pixels per foot
var paper = Raphael(0, 0, 500, 500),
```

```
    SCALE = 1,
    HOME_PLATE = { x: 250, y: 350 },
    FOUL_POLE = 250;
```

Of course, SVG graphics are meant to scale without us hard-coding a scaling factor. I find it convenient to define one in the code for situations like this, where there is an explicit scale between the screen and a real world object, whether it's a stadium or a solar system. We can always scale the whole graphic again down the road if need be.

You'll notice I use some uppercase variables. This is a personal convention of mine in JavaScript that I reserve for numerical values that are constant over the lifetime of the program, but that I may wish to alter by hand to change the specs of the graphic. It has no role whatsoever in determining how the program sees the variables. I've also stored the x and y coordinates of home plate in a simple object, rather than taking the time to write HOME_PLATE_X and HOME_PLATE_Y.

Okay, let's make a shape that outlines the field. To draw the foul lines, we'll start at the position of home plate and draw the line 250 pixels to the left field foul pole. This involves a little trigonometry.

The foul pole is 45 degrees to the left if you're standing on home plate facing the pitcher. JavaScript's trig functions need that in radians—that is, $\pi/4$.

```
var foul_line_left = "M" + HOME_PLATE.x + "," + HOME_PLATE.y + "l"
    + -1 * FOUL_POLE * Math.cos(Math.PI / 4) + ","
    + -1 * FOUL_POLE * Math.sin(Math.PI / 4);
```

Instead of hardcoding the numbers into the paths, as we did in the first examples, it's generally easier to compute the strings you'll pass to Raphael by making a string from numerical variables and the required function, as above. If you're used to "strongly typed" languages like Java or Python, which throw an error when you try to add variables of different types, this will look like trouble. JavaScript is "weakly typed," so it's fine with adding numbers to strings, converting them to text in the process.

(Not that we make the x and y distances after the lowercase "l" negative because we're going left and up relative to home base.)

Now let's draw an arc along the outfield fence to the other foul pole:

```
var outfield_fence = "a" + FOUL_POLE + "," + FOUL_POLE + " 0 0,1 "
    + 2 * HOME_PLATE.x * Math.sin(Math.PI / 4) + "," + 0;
```

We're using the foul pole distance as the radius, meaning home plate will form the center of the circular ellipse describing the fence. We do not want to take the long route, so we set the first flag to 0, but we do want to go clockwise, so we set the second one to 1.

Last, we'll draw a line back to where we started, using the capital L for convenience:

```
var foul_line_right = "L" + HOME_PLATE.x + "," + HOME_PLATE.y;
```

```
var field = paper.path(foul_line_left + outfield_fence + foul_line_right)
    .attr({ stroke: "none", fill: "green" });
```

Looking good so far, though the center field fence looks a little close to me. We can remedy this by extending the second radius in the arc:

```
var outfield_fence = "a" + FOUL_POLE + "," + 1.5 * FOUL_POLE + " 0 0,1 "
    + 2 * HOME_PLATE.x * Math.sin(Math.PI / 4) + "," + 0;

var field = paper.path(foul_line_left + outfield_fence + foul_line_right)
    .attr({ stroke: "none", fill: "green" });
```

Much better. Now let's make a square infield representing the basepaths and put some bases on it. To do so, we could make a path that starts at home and then goes 90 feet (pixels) northwest, then northeast, then southeast, then back to home. That would involve a lot of trig. I have a better idea that harkens back to Chapter 2: let's just draw a square and rotate it into position.

First we'll construct the infield using home plate as an origin and not worrying about rotation. This handy HTML color table (*http://bit.ly/html-colors*) suggests that #993300 is a nice dirt color.

```
var infield = paper.set();

infield.push(paper.rect(HOME_PLATE.x, HOME_PLATE.y, 90, 90)
    .attr({stroke: "none", fill:            "#993300"}));

infield.attr("transform", "R-135 " + HOME_PLATE.x + " " + HOME_PLATE.y);
```

For the bases, I'm going to make a loop that iterates four times and draws a base on each corner. (Yes, we're cheating and make home plate a square, but you do have the capacity to draw one using paths for extra credit.)

```
//bases
for (var c = 0; c < 4; c += 1) {
    infield.push(paper.rect(HOME_PLATE.x + 85 * (c % 2), HOME_PLATE.y + 85
 * (c >= 2), 5, 5)
        .attr({stroke: "none", "fill": "white"}));
}
```

Note that 85 * (c / 2 >= 1) make use of the fact that a true/false statement resolves to zero or one.

To swing the infield into place, we'll rotate it 135 degrees, using home plate as the pivot point:

```
infield.attr("transform", "R-135 " + HOME_PLATE.x + " " + HOME_PLATE.y);
```

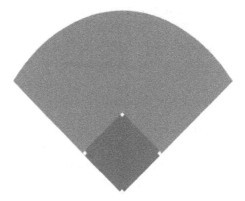

See this code live on jsFiddle (*http://jsfiddle.net/raphaeljs/46JJu/*).

Beautiful! Of course, a real baseball field is much more refined, with dirt extending in a radius from the pitcher's mound, grass in foul territory, and so forth. I'll leave it as an exercise to the ambitious reader to extend this example. The point is, there is nothing about a baseball diagram that you cannot replacate with your current Raphael toolset.

Final Thoughts

You might be thinking: Wait, why did I mess around with all that trigonometry if I could have drawn the entire field on its side, with the left-field foul line perfectly horizontal, and then rotated the field 45 degrees, not unlike the strategy for drawing the diamond? To that I respond: Please file all complaints by snail mail.

Actually, that's a fantastic idea. In fact, that's precisely what engineers do all the time, applying a transformation to a dataset that makes it easier to work with. Both ways work, and the best route is always the one that you're able to best visualize and understand. People who think more conceptually might like to draw the lines in the locations that they will ultimately appear. Those who think geometrically might prefer to draw something on its side, where diagonal lines become straight lines, and then rotate it. Coding is a collaborative process between your mind and the computer's mind, and happy programmers are ones who find the ideal meeting point.

Animations, Part One

At some point in your career as a Raphaelite, you will probably discover that, like the Greek sculptor Pygmalion, you are so enamored with your creation that you wish it could become a living being. Pygmalion had to invoke the help of Venus. We only need to use animations.

We already have plenty of practice changing the properties of our objects, whether it's altering their color or applying a transformation when the user clicks them. Animations do not introduce any fundamentally new concepts; they merely instruct Raphael to take its time getting from A to B.

The Basics

First, let's dial up our pal the red dot.

```
var paper = Raphael(0, 0, 500, 500);
var dot = paper.circle(50, 50, 20).attr({ "fill": "red" });
```

Next, we'll instantiate a new animation, which takes two arguments (for now): an object representing a series of properties we would like our element to have at the end of its journey, and the number of milliseconds it should take to reach this state.

```
var anim = Raphael.animation({ cx: 100, cy: 200, fill: "blue" }, 1000);
```

Note that `dot` is not referenced anywhere here. Like functions that can manipulate a wide variety of objects, animations exist independently of elements. We could apply this new animation to anything we like, though it won't make much sense for elements that do not have a `cx` or `cy` property.

To connect the two, we feed `anim` to the `.animate()` method of our dot:

```
dot.animate(anim);
```

See this code live on jsFiddle (*http://jsfiddle.net/raphaeljs/LeZ2Y/*).

Fire this up and you will see the red dot travel to the coordinates (100,200) and turn blue over the course of one second.

Another thing to note is that `animation()` is a function attached to the global object Raphael, not a method of the `paper` instance that we typically declare on the first line of any project. It's easy to mess this up early in your Raphael journey, before the distinction is clear. Functions that are methods of `paper`, like `.circle()` or `.path()`, return objects that have a physical representative on the page, and thus need to be associated with a specific canvas. `Raphael.animation()` does not make a new element. It just sets the stage for a manipulate once fed to the `paper.animate()` method.

Animation objects like `anim` have two methods of their own: `.delay()` and `.repeat()`. The first takes an input of milliseconds that cause the animation to wait before firing, while the second takes an integer for the number of times the animation should loop. You can call these functions either when declaring an animation:

```
var paper = Raphael(0, 0, 500, 500);
var square = paper.rect(50, 50, 100, 25).attr({ "fill": "green" });
var anim = Raphael.animation({x: 100, y: 200, height: 125}, 750).delay(1000);

// causes square to sit around for 1 second before animating
square.animate(anim);
```

...or when feeding it to an element:

```
var paper = Raphael(0, 0, 500, 500);
var anim = Raphael.animation({x: 100, y: 200, height: 125}, 750);

// causes square to sit around for 1 second before animating
square.animate(anim.repeat(2));
```

Charmingly, `.repeat()` even understands a value of `Infinity` as an input, though the processor on the computer is likely to blow before time ends.

Getting There is Half the Fun

Right now, the shapes that we're animating move with a constant velocity, i.e., after half the duration we've specified, they are halfway there. We'd needn't be so stiff! Raphael offers a variety of *easing formulas* that specify different tempos for the animation.

Think of it like driving to the house of a friend who lives 40 miles away. Let's say you have to be there in exactly an hour, just in time to participate in a surprise party but not so early as to ruin said surprise. The simplest thing to do is set your cruise control to 40 miles an hour. But of course, your residential neighborhood, overpopulated as it is with dogs and children, frowns upon that sort of behavior. More likely, you will go 20 mph for a few minutes, 40 mph for a bit longer, 65 mph on the interstate, and then back to 40 mph after getting off the interstate. You will glide into her driveway at a mild 10 mph, arriving at the exact same time as if you'd gone 40 mph the whole way.

Similarly, easing formulas do not alter the total time it takes an animation to complete, only how much progress it has made at incremental points in between.

To use an easing formula, you feed the animation a string as its third argument. The default easing formulas are linear, easeIn, easeOut, easeInOut, backIn, backOut, elastic, and bounce. Let's see what a few of them look like.

```
var paper = Raphael(0, 0, 500, 500);
var dot = paper.circle(50, 50, 20).attr({ "fill": "red" });

// let's make a little more room so as to have time to see the full effect
var anim = Raphael.animation({cx: 200, cy: 300, fill: "blue" }, 1000, "easeIn");
dot.animate(anim);
```

Here, we see the animation start slowly and then speed up. (Perhaps you overdid it on caution driving the first leg of your trip and have to floor it to get there on time.)

Here's a fun one:

```
var paper = Raphael(0, 0, 500, 500);
var dot = paper.circle(50, 50, 20).attr({ "fill": "red" });

// let's make a little more room so as to have time to see the full effect
var anim = Raphael.animation({cx: 200, cy: 300, fill: "blue" }, 1000,
"backOut");
dot.animate(anim);
```

Here, you missed the exit, went too far, and had to turn around at the end. But you still made it in exactly an hour!

Playing around with the different easing formulas makes for a fun 15 minutes. A little bit later in this chapter, we'll learn how to make our own.

Being There is the Other Half of the Fun

Adding to the above example, let's paste a message to the screen celebrating the completion of the animation:

```
var paper = Raphael(0, 0, 500, 500);
var square = paper.rect(50, 50, 100, 25).attr({ "fill": "red" });

var anim = Raphael.animation({x: 100, y: 200, height: 125}, 1000, "easeIn");
square.animate(anim);

alert("We've arrived!");
```

Whoops! That doesn't work at all; the message pops up immediately after the square takes off. This is because of an essential point for animations: life goes on everywhere else on the page while the animation is taking place. And we should be thankful for it, because otherwise it would be impossible to have any sort of concurrent activity on the page, such as two balls bouncing or two characters barrelling toward their confrontation.

Imagine how dull Super Mario Brothers would be if Mario and the Goombas took turns moving! Of course, deep inside the machine, everyone is taking turns—we're not talking about parallel processors here. The effect, however, is of simultaneous movement.

Fortunately, `Raphael.animate()` accepts a function as a final argument that gets called only after the animation is complete. Let's try this the right way:

```
var paper = Raphael(0, 0, 500, 500);
var square = paper.rect(50, 50, 100, 25).attr({ "fill": "red" });

function whenDone() {
    alert("We've arrived!");
}

var anim = Raphael.animation({x: 100, y: 200, height: 125}, 1000, "easeIn",
whenDone);
square.animate(anim);
```

See this code live on jsFiddle (*http://jsfiddle.net/raphaeljs/wDbt3/*).

The function `whenDone` is known as a *callback* function, a non-technical term for functions that fire at the end of some event, since they call you back when something has finished happening. I never cared for this analogy, but it's the accepted term. If you're familiar with retrieving files using AJAX calls, this will look familiar (if not, no sweat). When getting a file from a server, you have to make sure the file comes back before you operate on it, so you attach a callback function to the request. Under the hood it's totally different, but the syntax is remarkably similar.

Of course, you don't always need all four arguments. You may want a callback function but be perfectly fine with the default linear easing. You could just write the word `eas ing` for the third argument, but that would be kind of a drag. Fortunately, Raphael is actually pretty smart about what you give it. If it gets a function for the third argument, it knows it's probably the callback function.

Animating Paths

You can animate the `path` property of a shape just like x, y, or any other property. Raphael has to do a little more work for us here to figure out what to do. Let's look at an example using our `NGon` function from the previous chapter.

```
var paper = Raphael(0, 0, 500, 500);

function NGon(x, y, N, side, angle) {
    paper.circle(x, y, 3).attr("fill", "black");

    var path = "",
        c, temp_x, temp_y, theta;

    for (c = 0; c <= N; c += 1) {
```

```
        theta = c / N * 2 * Math.PI;
        temp_x = x + Math.cos(theta) * side;
        temp_y = y + Math.sin(theta) * side;
        path += (c === 0 ? "M" : "L") + temp_x + "," + temp_y;
    }
    return path;
}

var pentagon_path = NGon(50, 50, 5, 20);
var decagon_path = NGon(50, 50, 10, 20);

var shape = paper.path(pentagon_path);
var anim = Raphael.animation({ path: decagon }, 1000);

agon.animate(anim);
```

See this code live on jsFiddle (*http://jsfiddle.net/raphaeljs/X966n/*).

There are some good things and some bad things going on here. The good thing is that the shape successfully animates from a five-sided one to a ten-side one over the course of one second, like we asked. The bad thing is that it achieves several advanced yoga poses in the process. This is because, unlike moving something from one point to another, there's no single obvious way to transform one shape into another—even when it's a simple as doubling the number of sides in an object. When assigned the task, Raphael first matches the old path and the new path point by point, then tacks on any extra points in the new path to the end.

In a perfect world, Raphael might be able to interpolate a little and add the new points between the existing ones when appropriate. The world being imperfect, we can help it out by packing in the extra points that we're going to need later.

Let's practice by making a second function, N2Gon, which doubles up on the points:

```
var paper = Raphael(0, 0, 500, 500);

function NGon(x, y, N, side, angle) {
    //same as above
}

function N2Gon(x, y, N, side, angle) {
    var path = "",
        c, temp_x, temp_y, theta;

    // double up on points by iterating twice, using Math.floor(c/2)
    // e.g. 0,0,1,1,2,2
    for (c = 0; c <= 2*N; c += 1) {
        theta = Math.floor(c / 2) / N * 2 * Math.PI;
        temp_x = x + Math.cos(theta) * side;
        temp_y = y + Math.sin(theta) * side;
        path += (c === 0 ? "M" : "L") + temp_x + "," + temp_y;
    }
```

```
        return path;
    }

    var pentagon = N2Gon(50, 50, 5, 20);
    var decagon = NGon(50, 50, 10, 20);

    var agon = paper.path(pentagon);
    var anim = Raphael.animation({ path: decagon }, 1000);
    agon.animate(anim);
```

See this code live on jsFiddle (*http://jsfiddle.net/raphaeljs/pLPTU/*).

Much better! That pentagon makes a beautiful transition to a decagon. It works pretty well even if you boost the decagon to a twelve-sided shape (whatever that's called).

Generally speaking, when animating paths you want the original shape and the new shape to have the same number of points, or as close to it as possible, even if it means packing a few superfluous points in at one end or the other.

Piecewise Animations

After a while, going straight from point A to point B gets tiresome. You might want to bounce a ball off of a brick wall, which requires an abrupt change of direction halfway through the animation.

To do this, we of course need to start with a brick wall. Brick walls do not animate as a matter of policy, but I think we ought to seize this opportunity to practice:

```
    var paper = Raphael(0, 0, 500, 500);

    function brickwall(x, y, width, height, bricks) {
        var h = height / bricks,
            w = width / 3,
            props = { fill: "firebrick", stroke: "#CCC" };

        for (var b = 0; b < bricks; b += 1) {
            // we'll stick these at 0,0 for now and arrange them in a sec
            var shortbrick = paper.rect(0, 0, w, h).attr(props);
            var longbrick = paper.rect(0, 0, 2 * w, h).attr(props);
            // alternate brick patterns
            if (b % 2) {
                shortbrick.transform("T" + x + "," + (y + b * h));
                longbrick.transform("T" + (x + w) + "," + (y + b * h));
            } else {
                longbrick.transform("T" + x + "," + (y + b * h));
                shortbrick.transform("T" + (x + 2 * w) + "," + (y + b * h));
            }
        }
    }

    brickwall(300, 20, 40, 300, 30);
```

The idea is to have the ball bounce off the wall. So we have to animate it two times, once to get to the wall, once to get away from it.

```
var ball = paper.circle(50, 50, 10).attr("fill", "orange");

//send it to x coord 290 (the wall is at 300, the radius of the ball is 10)
var animToWall = Raphael.animation({ cx: 290, cy: 150 }, 500);
var animAwayFromWall = Raphael.animation({ cx: 50, cy: 250 }, 500);
```

We learned the hard way a few pages back that you can't just do this:

```
ball.animate(animToWall);
ball.animate(animAwayFromWall);
```

Raphael doesn't wait for one animation to finish before firing off the next, so this won't work. But we can make use of callback functions to fix that:

```
var animAwayFromWall = Raphael.animation({ cx: 50, cy: 250 }, 1000);
var animToWall = Raphael.animation({ cx: 292, cy: 150 }, 1000, function() {
    this.animate(animAwayFromWall);
});
ball.animate(animToWall);
```

Once again, that's much better. But we can imagine it getting tiresome if we have more than one brick wall in there. Fortunately, there is a rather poorly documented feature of Raphael that allows us to pack several stages into one animation. You can accomplish the same thing like this:

```
var anim = Raphael.animation({
    "50%": { cx: 292, cy: 150 },
    "100%": { cx: 50, cy: 250 }
}, 2000);

ball.animate(anim);
```

See this code live on jsFiddle (*http://jsfiddle.net/raphaeljs/dpB2f/*).

The percentages refer to the progress through the animation and indicate at which point it switches over from one animation to the next. If you'd like the ball to lose a little velocity on impact, just change the first value to 40% so that it gets there faster.

Case Study: Metronome

For many of us, an old-school mechanical metronome evokes cherished memories of practicing scales on the piano, usually at gunpoint. In those pre-Raphaelite days, metronomes were made of metal and wound by hand. The tempo was controlled by an adjustable weight along the arm of the metronome (this is known as an inverted pendulum).

For the sake of nostalgia, and armed with the power of animations, I propose we make a metronome of our own. Like the dominoes example, we're going to make an object to contain the Raphael elements and return methods to control it.

Since I'm not exactly sure what specifications I'll need, I'm going to pass only one argument to the metronome function, called opts. This is an object that will contain properties like height and position. This has the advantage of not requiring us to remember the order of the arguments in the function.

```
var metronome = function(opts) {
    // if no options specified, make an empty object
    opts = opts || {};

    //default values for variables if unspecified
    var len = opts.len || 200, // length of metronome arm
        angle = opts.angle || 20, //max angle from upright
        width = len * Math.cos(angle),
        x = opts.x || 0,
        y = opts.y || 0,
        tempo = 100;

    // pieces of the metronome
    var arm = paper.path("M" + (x + width) + "," + y + "v" + len).attr({
```

```
        'stroke-width': 5,
        stroke: "#999"
});

    var weight = paper.path("M" + (x+width) + ","   + (y+len) +
"h9l3,-18h-24l3,18h12")
        .attr({
            'stroke-width': 0,
            fill: '#666'
        });


    /* Next, let's set the weight at the center of the arm, make a label for
the tempo, and use a drag event to allow the user to adjust the tempo by moving
it. */

    //start the weight at the halfway point (18px less than length bc of weight)
    weight.position = (len - 18) / 2;
    weight.transform("T0,-" + weight.position);

    var label = paper.text(x + width, y + len + 15, tempo);

    // track drag position
    var drag_position;

    weight.drag(
        function(x, y, dx, dy, e) {
            // restrict weight to top of bar and very bottom, allowing for 18px
            // height of weight
            drag_position = Math.min(len - 18, Math.max(0, this.position - y));

            // calculate tempo based on position, with range of 20 to 180 bpm
            tempo = Math.round(20 + 160 * drag_position / (len - 18));
            label.attr("text", tempo);
            this.transform('T0,-' + drag_position);
        },
        function(x, y, e) {
            this.attr("fill", "#99F");
        },
        function(e) {
            this.position = drag_position;
            this.attr("fill", "#666");
        }
    );
}
```

If the use of `drag_position` is confusing here, consult "Better Dragging" on page 36.

Let's see how it looks so far:

```
var paper = Raphael(0, 0, 500, 500);
metronome({
    x: 125,
    y: 20,
    len: 240
});
```

100

Slide that weight up and down and you'll see the tempo adjust accordingly. Now we need to make it play. To do so, we're going to return a function called play to set off the metronome. This will go at the end of the function.

Inside the play function, we're going to be animating the transform property, which means we'll need two animations: one for the arm and one for the weight, since their transformations are different. They will be three-part animations: a half tick to the right, a full tick to the left, and a half tick back to center. Thus, a full animation represents two ticks of the metronome: Once there, once back.

```
return {
    play: function(repeats) {

        var armAnim = {
            "25%": { transform:"R" + angle + " " + (x+width) + "," + (y+len),
easing: "sinoid" },
            "75%": { transform:"R-" + angle + " " + (x+width) + "," + (y+len),
easing: "sinoid" },
            "100%": { transform:"R0 " + (x + width) + "," + (y + len), easing:
"sinoid" }
        };

        var weightAnim = {
            "25%": { transform:"T0,-" + weight.position + "R" + angle + " "
                + (x + width) + "," + (y + len), easing: "sinoid" },
            "75%": { transform:"T0,-" + weight.position + "R-" + angle + " "
                + (x + width) + "," + (y + len), easing: "sinoid" },
            "100%": { transform:"T0,-" + weight.position + "R0 "
                + (x + width) + "," + (y + len), easing: "sinoid" }
```

```
        };

        //2 iterations per animation * 60000 ms per minute / tempo
        var interval = 120000 / tempo;
                arm.animate(Raphael.animation(armAnim, interval).repeat
            (repeats / 2));
                weight.animate(Raphael.animation(weightAnim, interval).
            repeat(repeats / 2));

    }
};
```

Last, let's add a button in the HTML to trigger the metronome. Make sure to give the container div a little height so that it doesn't cover up the button.

```
<input type="button" value="play" id="play" />
<div id="canvas"></div>
```

And we're all set:

```
var paper = Raphael("canvas", 500, 500);
function metronome { /* all of the above */ }

var m = metronome({
    x: 125,
    y: 10,
    angle: 30,
    len: 240
});

document.getElementById("play").onclick = function() {
    m.play(10);
}
```

Each time you click the play button, you'll get 10 ticks of the metronome at the tempo specified by dragging the weight.

See this code live on jsFiddle (*http://jsfiddle.net/raphaeljs/9b4WL/*).

Wait, Aren't You Forgeting Something?

Oh right, sound! Getting audio in a browser is a bit outside the scope of this book, though it's not too difficult (particularly if you decide only to support browsers that recognize the audio tag).

To add to this feature, you'd add the function to make the ticking a `callback` property in `armAnim`, like so:

```
var armAnim = {
    "25%": { transform:"R" + angle + " " + (x+width) + "," + (y+len), easing:
"sinoid", callback: function() { console.log("tick"); }},
    "75%": { transform:"R-" + angle + " " + (x+width) + "," + (y+len), easing:
"sinoid", callback: function() { console.log("tock"); }},
    "100%": { transform:"R0 " + (x + width) + "," + (y + len), easing: "si-
noid" }
};
```

Final Thoughts

Playing with animations is great fun in Raphael because it does so much of the work for you. Just specify the before and after photos and let the code worry about shedding all those pounds.

I probably wouldn't use Raphael for a feature-length animated movie, but I would—and do—use its animations to breathe a little life into an otherwise static-looking website. Even the five-page website I made for my wedding uses Raphael to write my name and that of my lovely fiancée in script across the screen, as though an invisible hand were practicing its (flawless) cursive. A little movement signals to viewers that this is not just another assemblage of JPGs. And when it responds to their mouse movement, as we now know how to do, they'll also realize it is not even another assemblage of GIFs.

CHAPTER 6

Maps, Illustrations, and Other Artifacts

I keep promising that Raphael is about more than revisiting memories of high school geometry (something that is always best accomplished with a therapist's supervision). Right now seems like a fine time to make good on that since we've covered all of the core skills for image manipulation.

Let's dive right in to what is, in my experience, the most common data visualization on the web: a map that can be recolored on demand to represent a geographical dataset. We'll start with a map of the United States, and then run over how this can be easily extended to any country you're interested in.

Maps

Geographic entities are represented in the browser just like any other shape, as a series of points connected by lines. Colorado, for example—to choose a rather easy one—looks like this:

```
var CO = paper.path("m 380,320.9l4.9,-86.3l-113.4,-12.6l-12.2,
87.9l 120.7,11.0z");
```

(We think of Colorado as a straight rectangle, but here it comes from a map that mimcs the curvature of the earth, hence the tilt.)

So did I memorize the coordinates for all 50 states and then type them in here by hand? Of course not! Like most good things, this comes from Wikipedia. But we don't want a map on Wikipedia. We want one on our own website. Let's talk about how to import that information into Raphael.

Importing SVGs Found in Nature

When it comes to finding structural data for visualizations on the Web, one can generally rely on these laws:

1. There is roughly a 100% chance the information exists for free.
2. There is roughly a 0% chance it's in the format you need it to be in.

Case in point. Wikipedia has a very fine "Blank Map of US States (*http://bit.ly/states-map*)" SVG file that contains all the coordinates we need:

We must reverse-engineer that SVG back into JavaScript code so that we can render it dynamically and then mess with it.

This is not, unfortunately, a feature that Raphael natively offers. If you're a JavaScript jock who enjoys parsing DOM structures—those people do exist—you could fairly easily write some code to load the SVG file dynamically on the page and extract the coordinates. If you're not, you're in luck: many fine tools, most of them open-source, exist to help us extract the coordinates from SVG files (my favorite is ReadySetRaphael (*http://readysetraphael.com/*)). Let's try it.

After downloading the SVG file from Wikipedia to my desktop, I went to ReadySetRaphael and uploaded it. A second later, I get 50-some lines of beautiful JavaScript that look like this:

```
var rsr = Raphael('rsr', '959', '593');

var HI = rsr.path("m 233.08751,519.30948  1.93993,-3.55655  2.26326,-0.32332
0.32332,0.8083 ...

HI.attr({id: 'HI',class: 'state','stroke-width': '0','stroke-opacity': '1',
'fill': '#000000'}).data('id', 'HI');

var AK = rsr.path("m 158.07671,453.67502 -0.32332,85.35713
1.6166,0.96996 3.07157,0.16166 1.45494,...

AK.attr({id: 'AK',class: 'state','stroke-width': '0','stroke-opacity':
'1','fill': '#000000'}).data('id', 'AK');

//and so forth
```

I've obviously truncated the lines here, but this is looking good. ReadySetRaphael is even smart enough to figure out what to name the variables based on the ids of the SVG elements. You can paste all of this code into a page with the Raphael library loaded, add a <div id=*rsr*></div> to contain the objects, and you will get this:

See this code live on jsFiddle (*http://jsfiddle.net/raphaeljs/mNdmD/*).

If your goal was to make a JavaScript commentary on the dire state of America by coloring it all black, congratulations—you're done! If not, read on.

I sized this screenshot down to fit on the page, but in reality it's about 950 pixels wide, just like the original. As you can see, ReadySetRaphael is imperfect, since it didn't preserve the gray coloring of the original. But it's still a phenomenally useful tool. The first $10 in profits for *RaphaelJS*, if there are any, are going straight to this site's donation page.

Imperfect though it may be, we can work with this. We can even load it in Internet Explorer 8 and see the SVG we downloaded render in VML. Now that it's rendered on the page, it has entered our sphere of influence.

Manipulating SVGs Found in Nature

There are a few things I don't love about the raw JavaScript we get from ReadySetRaphael. It takes the liberty of making a new master Raphael object, rsr, but in reality we probably already made one. It also declares a new variable for every state. Generally speaking, you don't want to pollute the page with lots of variable names, particularly if there are other JavaScript libraries outside of your control firing off left and right. (For all you know, the web analytics script has a PA variable for "page analysis", or whatever, that will get overwritten by Pennsylvania.) But I also don't want to do a lot of work editing the raw output of ReadySetRaphael, since I'd like to be able to use it often and with minimal tedium. So I'm going to do something a little clever: delete the first line, which declares rsr, then wrap the entire thing in a function, which consigns all the variables to the function's scope, and pass that function an object called rsr:

```
function drawUS(rsr) {

    var HI = rsr.path("m 233.08751,519.30948 1.93993,-3.55655 2.26326,-0.32332
0.32332,0.8083 ...

        HI.attr({id: 'HI',class: 'state','stroke-width': '0','stroke-opacity':
'1','fill': '#000000'}).data('id', 'HI');

    var AK = rsr.path("m 158.07671,453.67502 -0.32332,85.35713 1.6166,0.96996
3.07157,0.16166 1.45494,...

        AK.attr({id: 'AK',class: 'state','stroke-width': '0','stroke-opacity':
'1','fill': '#000000'}).data('id', 'AK');
    // etc etc
}
```

This allows me to do this:

```
var paper = Raphael(0, 0, 1000, 600);

drawUS(paper);
```

If you don't like all those coordinates in the body of your program—I sure don't—you can just stick it in a file like usmap.js and call it after you summon Raphael.

This leaves us with a bit of a problem, however, because we don't really have a way to get the states back in order to resize and recolor them. We could crawl the DOM to relocate them, but that would completely defeat the purpose of Raphael. What we need is to add them all to a set.

I suppose we could take all that JavaScript from ReadySetRaphael and perform an elaborate find-and-replace command. As a rule, I like to avoid this sort of thing because it's tedius and it's hard to remember how to do the next time. Once again, there's a Raphael command to help out. It's called .setStart(), and until this very moment I never thought I'd see the day it was useful.

When you call paper.setStart(), it begins "recording" and adds every new element defined after that point to a set up until you call .setFinish(). The assignment for the set occurs at the end, like so:

```
var paper = Raphael(0, 0, 1000, 600);

paper.setStart();

drawUS(paper);

var mymap = paper.setFinish();
```

I don't like this syntax much. In fact, I suspect it exists to make people coming from Flash and ActionScript feel more at home. But it's really our easiest option at this point.

Now that we have all the states in one set, we can manipulate them. Let's try and recolor the map and resize it down by half, with brazen disregard for whether it will work:

```
mymap.attr({
    fill: "pink",
    transform: "S0.5,0.5"
});
```

I see two problems. There are some strange triangles getting filled in around Hawaii and Alaska. Also, all of the states are in the wrong place. These are both problems we can handle.

Those rogue lines are pretty easy to find in the source from ReadySetRaphael since they don't have a proper name:

```
var path57 = rsr.path("m 211,493 v 55 l 36,45 M 0,425 h 144 l 67,68 h 86 l
53,54 v 46"); path57.attr({id: 'path57',fill: 'none',stroke: '#a9a9a9',"stroke-
width": '2','stroke-opacity': '1'}).data('id', 'path57');
```

Let's delete them.

The other problem stems from the fact that we did not provide an anchor for the scaling, forcing Raphael to choose one for us. Raphael chose the center of each state. As you may recall, that's best remedied by adding two more coordinates to the transformation string:

```
mymap.attr({
    fill: "pink",
    transform: "S0.5,0.5,0,0"
});
```

Much better:

See this code live on jsFiddle (*http://jsfiddle.net/raphaeljs/5Huz5/*)

Now to add some data.

Adding Information

I would like to visualize the unemployment rate for each state, according to the Bureau of Labor Statistics (*http://1.usa.gov/un-rates*)—a problem you'll never have to deal with after becoming a Raphael master. You can visualize anything you want, but it's your job to organize that data so that every number is associated with a two-letter state abbre-viation. Believe it or not, the United States government doesn't offer the information in a neat JSON format, so I copied the information from BLS by hand and delimited it with a | character. There are better ways to do it, but this is fine:

```
var rates = {};

// split the data into tab-delimited pairs of abbreviations and numbers
var data = "ND    3|SD  3.9|NE  4.2|HI  4.5|UT  4.6|VT  4.6|WY  4.6|IA  4.8|NH
5.1|MN  5.2|MT  5.3|OK  5.3|VA  5.7|KS  5.9|WV  6.2|AL  6.3|AK  6.3|TX  6.5|ID
6.6|WI  6.8|ME  6.9|NM  6.9|WA  6.9|LA  7|CO   7.1|FL  7.1|MD  7.1|MO  7.1|MA
7.2|OH  7.2|AR  7.4|DE  7.4|NY  7.5|PA  7.5|AZ  8|OR   8|CT   8.1|SC  8.1|IN
8.4|KY  8.5|MS  8.5|TN  8.5|DC  8.6|NJ  8.6|CA  8.7|GA  8.8|MI  8.8|NC  8.9|RI
8.9|IL  9.2|NV  9.5".split("|");

// stick each value into an object with the state as the key
for (var c = 0; c < data.length; c += 1) {
    rates[data[c].split("\t")[0]] = parseFloat(data[c].split("\t")[1]);
}
```

We're almost done. The last thing we need is a color scheme (for which I always go to ColorBrewer2 (*http://colorbrewer2.org/*)) plus a calculation to translate the number into a shade. Then we'll simply loop through the states, find the right data point, and color it accordingly. ReadySetRaphael has helpfully assigned the id value of each original SVG object to the .data() property we previously covered, so it's easy to get back.

```
var colors =
["#f7fcf0","#e0f3db","#ccebc5","#a8ddb5","#7bccc4","#4eb3d3",
"#2b8cbe","#08589e"];

// iterate through the states
for (var i = 0; i < mymap.length; i += 1) {
    // retrieve the state abbreviation from the object
    var abbr = mymap[i].data('id');
    var unemp_rate = rates[abbr];

    // transform the rate (which varies from 3 to 9.5)
    // into a 0-7 index for the color array
    var index = Math.round(unemp_rate) - 3;
    var color = colors[index];
    mymap[i].attr("fill", color);
}
```

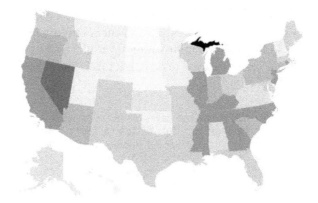

The only thing I see wrong here is that Michigan's Upper Peninsula has seceded from the United States. ReadySetRaphael got a little confused here and gave it the id SP, for what, I have no idea. Change that data value to MI and you'll be just fine. I'll spare you yet another screenshot.

See this code live on jsFiddle (*http://jsfiddle.net/raphaeljs/f9SaX/*).

Interlude: Raphael vs. D3

What we've done here is informally bind a dataset to collection of visual objects—the basic, holy work of data visualization. This is not necessarily the core purpose of Raphael, but it is, in my experience, its most utilitarian use.

It *is* the core purpose of D3, which, after all, stands for "data-driven documents." If your ambition is to do lots of sophisticated data projects, you may eventually discover that D3 is worth the extra effort and steeper learning curve (I use it all the time for more stats-heavy projects). If you do, you'll heartily thank me for starting you off this way, because the concept is nearly identical: you're taking data and using it to guide the color, shape, or location of an object on the screen.

The vast majority of mapping projects, however, do not require industrial-level Java-Script. For those, the approach outlined in this chapter works beautifully in all browsers.

Case Study: Paint by Numbers

Many sites allow you to customize a little cartoon avatar to represent yourself in your transactions, and we're nearly at the point where that's possible purely with Raphael. This demo is going to allow you to recolor any SVG you like right in the browser.

The first thing we'll need is a color palette. There are many sophisticated plug-ins you can download and use, often in conjunction with jQuery, but for our purposes I think we should build our own.

For that, I'd like to introduce a handy Raphael function called .hsl(), which stands for "hue, saturation, lightness." It's an alternative to the more common RGB system of representing colors in the browser, and accepts three values from zero to one.

It's convenient for us here because we can create a range of colors for our selector in a loop. This is best explained with an example:

```
var paper = Raphael(0, 0, 500, 500);
var colors = paper.set();

for (var c = 0; c < 16; c += 1) {
    for (var i = 0; i < 3; i += 1) {
        colors.push(
            paper.rect(10 + c * 20, 10 + i * 20, 20, 20)
                .attr({
                    fill: Raphael.hsl(c / 16, 1, (i+1)/4),
                    stroke: "#CCC"
                })
        );
    }
}
```

This pair of nested loops creates 48 (16 × 3) colors of a range of shades and lightnesses, all with full saturation:

To complete my color pickers, I'm going to make a big box to represent the currently selected color and add an event listener to the smaller ones to update the selected value when clicked:

```
var selected_color = "red";
var selected_color_box = paper.rect(10 + 17 * 20, 10, 60, 60).attr({
    fill: "red",
    stroke: "#CCC"
});

colors.click(function() {
    selected_color = this.attr("fill");
    //reset all borders to gray
    colors.attr("stroke", "#CCC").attr("stroke-width", 1);
    //set selected color's border to heavier black.
    //bring to front so wider stroke width isn't clipped by neighbors
    this.attr("stroke", "#000").attr("stroke-width", 2).toFront();
    //update the big box
    selected_color_box.attr("fill", selected_color);
});
```

See this code live on jsFiddle (*http://jsfiddle.net/chriswilsondc/zszAZ/6/*).

This modest tool leaves something to be desired (like black, white and gray), but it's not bad for a minute's work.

Now we're going to add an SVG from the Internet. I'm choosing a picture of a scientist (*http://www.clker.com/clipart-2446.html*) from Clker, my favorite royalty-free clip art site, but you can choose absolutely any SVG you want.

After running the SVG through ReadySetRaphael, we need to once again wrap it in a function, set the `.setStart()` and `.setFinish()` functions to the beginning and end, and return that set, exactly as we did for the map.

```
function person(rsr) {
    rsr.setStart();
    // all the output from ReadySetRaphael
    return rsr.setFinish();
}

var scientist = person(paper);
```

Then, all we need to finish is a single event handler:

```
scientist.click(function() {
    // remember, "this" refers to the individual element clicked, not the whole
scientist
    this.attr("fill", selected_color);
});
```

Just like that, we can allow any visitor to our site to live-edit the colors of any SVG we provide. I'll leave you with the results of my own handiwork, which looks to me like nothing so much as a rejected idea for a Scooby Doo villain.

See this code live on jsFiddle (*http://jsfiddle.net/raphaeljs/DJLrW/*).

CHAPTER 7

Animations, Part Two

The animations we covered in Chapter 5 were basically ways of delaying our hard work. By feeding attributes through an animation, we instruct Raphael to take its sweet time altering the appearance of an object instead of changing it all at once. That suits us just fine a lot of the time, but it can get dull. When moving an object to a different point in space, for example, we're currently only able to send it there in a straight line. And *RaphaelJS* takes a strong stance against that sort of unadventurous attitude.

Before we get too funky, however, I'd like to briefly touch upon the straightforward subject of how you can add your own functions and properties to Raphael, which will come in handy.

Extending Raphael

In Chapter 4, we ginned up a function called NGon to make regular polygons of any number of sides (of three or more). The function accepted coordinates for the center of the shape, the length of each side of the shape, and number of sides. It returned a path string which we were responsible for feeding to paper.path().

That worked fine, but it would be nice to be able to use NGon alongside circle, rect, and the rest of the beloved crew. You could add this function to the source code, but this is generally a horrible way to do things because it runs a high risk of messing something else up and gets overwritten every time we update Raphael. Fortunately, Raphael offers an object called Raphael.fn that allows us to *extend* its out-of-the-box functions.

Adding Functions

To add a function, assign a function to `Raphael.fn` as though it were an object (which it is):

```
Raphael.fn.NGon = function(x, y, N, side) {
    var path = "", n, temp_x, temp_y, angle;
    for (n = 0; n <= N; n += 1) {
        console.log(n);
        angle = n / N * 2 * Math.PI;
        temp_x = x + Math.cos(angle) * side;
        temp_y = y + Math.sin(angle) * side;
        path += (n === 0 ? "M" : "L") + temp_x + "," + temp_y;
    }
    // "this" refers to the paper object that called the function
    var shape = this.path(path);
    // don't forget to return the shape so that you can access it later
    return shape;
}
var paper = Raphael(0, 0, 500, 500);

paper.NGon(40, 40, 3, 30);
paper.NGon(100, 80, 7, 20);
```

It's not a huge difference, but it's significantly more elegant. And this trick will come in handy in just a moment.

Adding Attributes

Most of the attributes you can assign to an element in Raphael map directly to the SVG specifications. If you state `thing.attr("fill", "#FF0000")`, it makes that thing red. If you were to inspect the element in the DOM after that command is run, you would see `fill="#FF0000"` as an attribute of the element.

You can't add anything to the SVG specification without petitioning the World Wide Web Consortium, which I would recommend against doing if you can help it. But if you want to invent an attribute that represents some combination of existing attributes, you can knock yourself out using `paper.customAttributes`. Whatever you add is a function that accepts a number and modifies the element accordingly:

```
var paper = Raphael(0, 0, 500, 500);
paper.customAttributes.redness = function (num) {
    var val = 255 * (1 - num / 100);
    // note that we do not directly operate on an object
    // instead, we return the object of final attributes
    return {fill: "rgb(255," + val + ", " + val + ")"};
};

paper.rect(10, 10, 50, 50).attr("redness", 50);
```

```
paper.circle(50, 50, 20).attr({
    redness: 25,
    'stroke-width': 3
});
```

Adding Methods

The third and final means of extending Raphael is to create methods that act on elements, the way `toFront()` rearranges an object in the DOM or `remove()` deletes it. Here's a function that makes an element more red than it was before:

```
Raphael.el.redder = function() {
    var rgb = Raphael.getRGB(this.attr("fill"));
    rgb.r += 51;
    this.attr("fill", "rgb(" + rgb.r + "," + rgb.g + "," + rgb.b + ")");
}
var paper = Raphael(0, 0, 500, 500);

// a sort of putrid olive color
var r1 = paper.rect(10, 10, 50, 50).attr("fill", "#999900");

// a putrid brown
var r2 = paper.rect(80, 10, 50, 50).attr("fill", "#999900").redder();

// a lovely orange
var r3 = paper.rect(150, 10, 50, 50).attr("fill", "#999900").redder().redder();
```

See this code live on jsFiddle (*http://jsfiddle.net/raphaeljs/gNdb7/*).

You can think of these three means of extending Raphael as operating on three different planes: the global `Raphael` object (`.fn`), the paper object (`.customAttributes`), and the element (`.el`).

Animating Along a Path

The goal of this section is to create an animation that follows a track chosen by us, so we need a nice path. Conveniently, we could also use a little practice with custom shape types. Let's multitask:

```
Raphael.fn.rosetta = function(x,y,rx,ry,N) {
    if (N == 0) {
        console.log("no dividing by zero, please"); return;
    }
    var angle = 360 / N; // negative values of N are fine
    var path = "M" + x + "," + y;

    for (var c = 0; c < N; c += 1) {
        // need angle for each leaf of rosetta in radians
        var theta = angle * c * Math.PI / 180;
        // coords of farthest point from center for this leaf
```

```
            var dx = x + 2 * rx * Math.cos(theta),
                dy = y + 2 * rx * Math.sin(theta);

            path += "A" + rx + "," + ry + " " + angle * c + " 1,1 " + dx + "," + dy;
            path += "A" + rx + "," + ry + " " + angle * c + " 1,1 " + x + "," + y;
        }
        var rosetta = paper.path(path);
        return rosetta;
    }
```

By now, you should be able to somewhat imagine what this will look like. But let's fire it off to be sure:

```
var paper = Raphael(0, 0, 500, 500);
var rose = paper.rosetta(120, 120, 55, 35, 6);
```

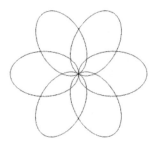

See this code live on jsFiddle (*http://jsfiddle.net/raphaeljs/TxHxs/*).

It's a thing of beauty! I'm not actually 100% sure this is technically a rosetta, but let's run with it.

Our goal is to make a shape that animates along the path of our rosetta, starting at the center and ending at the center. For that, we'll need a pair of extremely handy Raphael methods. The first is called `.getTotalLength()`, which returns the length in pixels of a path if it were to be unfurled into a straight line:

```
console.log(rose.getTotalLength());
// 1717.8...
```

If you check this mathematically by measuring the circumference of the ellipse and multiplying it by 6, which is a lot harder than I remember it being (the circumference, not the multiplication), you will see that it's very close.

The second method is `.getPointAtLength()`, which returns the x and y coordinates of any point along a path, taking as an argument a given number of pixels along that path. Let's try it will the point 800 pixels along the 1,717-pixel length of the rosetta:

```
var circle = paper.circle(0, 0, 10).attr("fill", "red");
var point = rosetta.getPointAtLength(800);
console.log(point);
// {x: 69.12, y: 139.84, alpha: 128.5 }
```

```
// don't worry about 'alpha' just yet

circle.attr({
    cx: point.x,
    cy: point.y
});
```

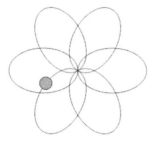

See this code live on jsFiddle (*http://jsfiddle.net/raphaeljs/9zTt8/*).

As you see, the red dot landed neatly on the rosetta at the right point.

All that's left is to animate it, though this is a tad trickier than it might seem. Remember that we have to animate *properties* like fill or transform. We could animate cx and cy, but this would mean the code we write will not work on anything other than a circle or an ellipse. So we're going to make a custom attribute called progress that represents a shape's progress through the path as a fraction from 0 to 1. It will return a transformation to move the animated shape to the correct point along the path.

But which path? Attributes typically operate on only the element to which they are applied, but in this case we need to supply a path as well. Since attributes don't take arguments the way functions do, we'll have to specify the path we'd like to automate along ahead of time:

```
circle.data("mypath", rose);

paper.customAttributes.progress = function (v) {
    var path = this.data("mypath");
    if (!path) {
        return {
            transform: "t0,0"
        };
    }
    var len = path.getTotalLength();
    var point = path.getPointAtLength(v * len);

    return {
        transform: "t" + point.x + "," + point.y
    };
};

circle.attr("progress", 0.3);
```

See this code live on jsFiddle (*http://jsfiddle.net/raphaeljs/EZSaC/*).

This successfully places the red dot 30% of the way along the complete path of six ellipses. (I originally tested it with 0.5, thought it didn't work, then realized that the 50% point along the path is the dead center.)

Now that this is working, let's give it a whirl with a nice long duration of 10 seconds.

```
circle.attr("progress", 0);
circle.animate({ progress: 1 }, 10000);
```

See this code live on jsFiddle (*http://jsfiddle.net/raphaeljs/jDThL/*).

I could watch that little red guy zip around the rosetta all day.

I mentioned that we shouldn't worry about `alpha` just yet. Now we can worry about it. In fact, it's quite an impressive feature; it returns the angle of the tangle line to the curve at the point specified. If you remember any calculus, it's the derivative at that point. If we want to make a shape that appears to "drive" around the path and adjust its direction accordingly, we can simply add a rotation to the transformation that the `progress` attribute returns. (I got the idea for this from the gear example (*http://raphaeljs.com/gear.html*) of the RaphaelJS website).

While we're at it, I'd like to test the object being animated for the presence of `width` and `height` attributes, which would indicate it's a shape whose coordinates refer to the upper-left corner instead of the center, and adjust accordingly to keep the shape's center point along the path:

```
paper.customAttributes.progress = function (v) {
    var path = this.data("mypath"),
        attrs = this.attr(),
        offset = { x: 0, y: 0 };

    if (!path) {
        return {
            transform: "t0,0"
        };
    }

    if (attrs.hasOwnProperty("width")) {
        offset.x = -this.attr("width") / 2;
        offset.y = -this.attr("height") / 2;
    }

    var len = path.getTotalLength();
    var point = path.getPointAtLength(v * len);
    return {
        transform: "t" + (point.x + offset.x) + "," + (point.y + offset.y) +
"r" + point.alpha
    };
};
```

```
var shape = paper.rect(0, 0, 20, 10).attr("fill", "green");
shape.data("mypath", rose);
shape.attr("progress", 0);
shape.animate({ progress: 1 }, 10000);
```

As a final feature, perhaps we might like to draw the path as we go instead of mapping out the course of the path ahead of time. If you're old enough to remember Logo, the old programming language for kids that ran on ancient Macs, this will look familiar.

To do so, we'll use a third convenience method from Raphael, `.getSubpath()`, which takes beginning and end lengths and returns just the portion of a path between those points.

Let's add this somewhere in the `progress` custom attribute:

```
var trail = this.data("mytrail");

if (trail) {
    // set the trail's path to just the amount current trespassed:
    trail.attr("path", path.getSubpath(0, v * len));
}
```

Here's a screenshot of our animation about a third of the way through.

See this code live on jsFiddle (*http://jsfiddle.net/raphaeljs/yzppk/*).

This is a particularly fun feature to use when animating letters. With nothing more than an SVG of written letters, you could make code to write out words on the screen as though a ghost where etching the letters in thin air (like in *Harry Potter*)!

Pause for Commentary

This all may seem like a bit of a hack. Why doesn't Raphael make it easier? In fact, there did used to be an `.animateAlong()` method that vanished in Raphael 2.0 for reasons I'm unclear on. But we don't need it. This is not a hack; it's merely a somewhat advanced usage of the many clever functions that Raphael offers out of the box. Rather than provide every possible tool, Raphael gives you just what you need to whet your imagination.

But you probably don't want to write a lot of code for every project. If any function you write seems useful and elegant enough for wider use, by you or anyone else, the `.fn`, `.el`, and `.customAttributes` functions allow you to store them in a JavaScript file and summon them on demand.

Custom Easing Formulas

Back in Chapter 5, we touched on the different easing formulas that Raphael offers, like `easeOut` and `backIn`. They're fun to play with, but eventually you may find yourself no longer entertained by the seven or eight options that come out of the box. Let's learn how to make our own.

The first thing to know about easing formulas is that they have no ability to change the final result of an animation. No matter what, your object will end up where it was going and always in the alloted time. In other words, animations are strictly Calvinist. Their destiny is written at birth.

The default easing formula, `linear`, maps the progress of the timer that's running over the course of the animation precisely to the progress of the shape in its journey to its destination. When the total time is 25% elapsed, the shape is 25% of the way to its final state. (I'm mainly thinking of animations through space here, but this applies to animations of any type.)

An easing formula is a function that excepts as an argument the progress of the animation in time as a fraction between 0 and 1 and returns the desired progress of the animation, also between 0 and 1. The default linear easing formula is just this:

```
function (n) {
    return n;
}
```

(I copied that from the Raphael source code.)

The `easeIn` formula, also known by Raphael as `ease-in` or `<`, looks like this:

```
function (n) {
    return pow(n, 1.7);
}
```

If you think this through a little, you'll see this has a dampening effect; the progress of the animation will lag behind the progress of the timer until the absolute last second, when it catches up. If this seems impossible, consider that the speed of the object, if it's moving through space, is the first derivative of the easing formula, and thus the shape lags in velocity at first and then speeds up to arrive on time.

If you're more of a visual thinker, here's a graph of the progress of the animation as a linear easing and an easeIn easing:

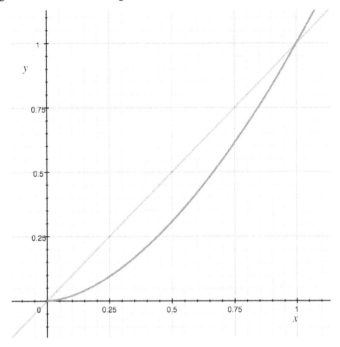

It's not a law of nature that the easing formula must neatly end up at a value of one. If it doesn't, however, you'll see an awkward skip at the very end as it jumps to its destination. (Remember, Calvinism: it ends up at 1 no matter what.)

The value that an easing formula returns can be negative or greater than one at some point in its lifetime. This is exactly what happens in the backOut and backIn formulas, which either start by going backward or overshooting the target and then backing in.

To make your own easing formula, assign a function with one argument to the object Raphael.easing_formula. Here's one I just made up:

```
var paper = Raphael(0, 0, 500, 500);
var square = paper.rect(20, 20, 30, 30).attr({ 'stroke-width': 0, fill:
"red" });

Raphael.easing_formulas.swing = function(n) {
    return n + Math.sin(n * Math.PI * 2) / 2;
};
square.animate({ transform: "t200,200" }, 2000, "swing");
```

Here's the visual representation of my swing easing formula:

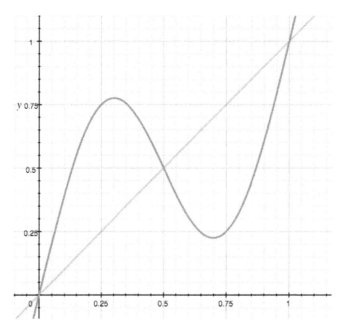

Give it a shot and you'll see the red square zip most of the way to its destination, change its mind and backtrack, and then get with the program and speed up to reach the final point on time.

Here's one that makes the square scatter around:

```
Raphael.easing_formulas.may_cause_seizures = function(n) {
    return n + 0.2 * Math.random() - 0.1;
};
square.animate({ transform: "t200,200" }, 2000, "may_cause_seizures");
```

See this code live on jsFiddle (*http://jsfiddle.net/raphaeljs/JGG7v/*).

You can see some more complex examples in the Raphael source code. Just look for the `easing_formulas` object.

Code Example: The Animated Solar System

Let's make a not-to-scale diorama of the first four planets in the solar system, and then animate the planets accordingly. The data we need is the average distance of each planet from the sun, the number of Earth days it takes to complete its orbit, and the eccentricity of the elliptical orbit—a geometric measure of how squashed it is. (An ellipse with an eccentricity of 1 is a circle; 0 would be a straight line.)

I found the dimensions for the orbits and the planets themselves and stuck them in a few objects for us.

```
var paper = Raphael(0, 0, 500, 450);

//http://nineplanets.org/data.html
var orbits = {
    Mercury: { distance: 57910, period: 87.97, eccen: 0.21 },
    Venus: { distance: 108200, period: 224.70, eccen: 0.01},
    Earth: { distance: 149600, period: 365.26, eccen: 0.02},
    Mars: { distance: 227940, period: 686.98, eccen: 0.09 }
};

//http://nineplanets.org/data1.html
var radii = {
    Sun: 695000,
    Mercury: 2440,
    Venus: 6052,
    Earth: 6378,
    Mars: 3397,
};

//chosen haphazardly
var colors = {
    Sun: "yellow",
    Mercury: "gray",
    Venus: "brown",
    Earth: "blue",
    Mars: "red"
}
```

We're going to take several large liberties here, even beyond eliminating the four outer planets.

```
// chose some scales by trial and error to get the solar sysem on the screen
var ORBIT_SCALE = 1.0 / 1000,
    PLANET_SCALE = 1.0 / 800;

//center at the middle of the canvas
var CENTER = {x: paper.width / 2, y: paper.height / 2};

// the sun needs extra scaling
var Sun = paper.circle(CENTER.x, CENTER.y, radii.Sun * PLANET_SCALE / 50)
    .attr("fill", colors.Sun);
```

Next, let's make a function to draw the planets and orbits and set up the animation. I won't belabor you too much with the geometry and astronomy, but we'll use the eccentricity to determine the distance between the center of the ellipse and the two foci of the ellipse. (This assumes you recognize Kepler, who tells us that the Sun is not at the center of the ellipitical orbit, but at one of the two foci. This is also not remotely proportional to the real orbits.)

```
var label_pos = 15;
function planet(name, data) {
    // calculate the long and short arms of the elliptical orbit
```

```
        // Also get focus from eccentricity of orbit
        // http://nineplanets.org/help.html#semim
        var perigee = data.distance * (1 - data.eccen) * ORBIT_SCALE,
            apogee = data.distance * (1 + data.eccen) * ORBIT_SCALE,
            focus = data.eccen * apogee,
            x = CENTER.x + focus - apogee,
            y = CENTER.y;

        // label for upper-left corner, where we'll record years elapsed
            var label = paper.text(10, label_pos, name + ": 0").attr("text-anchor",
    "start");
        label_pos += 20;

        // similar to rosetta leaf
        var path = "M" + x + "," + y;
        path += "a" + apogee + "," + perigee + " 0 1,1 " + apogee * 2 + ",0";
        path += "A" + apogee + "," + perigee + " 0 1,1 " + x + "," + y;

        var orbit = paper.path(path).attr({
            stroke: "gray",
            "stroke-dasharray": "--"
        });

        var body = paper.circle(0, 0, radii[name] * PLANET_SCALE).attr({
            fill: colors[name]
        });

        // assumes the custom attribute "progress" is defined same as above
        body.data("mypath", orbit);
        body.attr("progress", 0);

        var years_elapsed = 0;

        var anim = Raphael.animation({ progress: 1 }, MS_PER_DAY * orbits[name].pe-
    riod,
        function() {
            years_elapsed += 1;
            label.attr("text", name + ": " + years_elapsed);
        }).repeat(Infinity);

        body.animate(anim);
    }
```

Now all that's left is to loop through the objects and create the planets:

```
    for (var name in orbits) {
        planet(name, orbits[name]);
    }
```

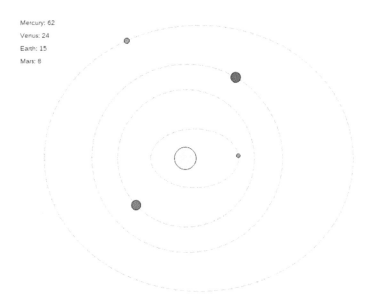

Mercury: 62
Venus: 24
Earth: 15
Mars: 8

See this code live on jsFiddle (*http://jsfiddle.net/raphaeljs/yQ6WF/*).

And there you have it: your second grade art class homework is complete.

CHAPTER 8

Mobile, Global Variables, and Other Things That Hurt Less Than You Think

Up until about a year ago, my strategy for dealing with people with mobile browsers was to pretend they didn't exist. This worked reasonably well. Alas, times change.

The number of viewers accessing a site from a phone or tablet varies dramatically depending on the type of site. For example, if you're working on the website for the Laptop Fan Club, this might not be a concern. In almost any other situation, it's something you have to deal with.

When it comes to visualizations, there are some practical decisions to be made about what's realistic on different screen sizes. A county-level map is not going to be all that informative on a 300-pixel screen. But in many cases, you do want a visual to resize dynamically to fit whatever size screen is loading it.

This is generically known as *responsive design*, and there are sophisticated libraries out there like Bootstrap (*http://getbootstrap.com*), an open-source project from Twitter that intelligently moves or hides parts of a page (like menus and sidebars) depending on the size of the screen. The idea is to code your website only once, not once for every type of device that might hypothetically access it.

Raphael predates the responsive design movement, but in fact scalable vector graphics are absolutely perfect for responsive design since they are, as you may have divined, scalable vectors. Since they're drawn dynamically, you don't have to worry about the nasty side effects you get when a photo that's supposed to be one size is squeezed into a smaller container. You just have to do a little extra work to make SVGs adjust to their surroundings.

Measuring the Container

Let's freshen up on dynamically resizing containers. The easiest way to do this is to use CSS to set the width of a block-level element, like a regular old `<div>`, to 100% (or any other percent you like).

You can then measure the width of the element by finding it with JavaScript and retrieving the `offsetWidth` property.

```
<style>
#canvas {
    width: 100%;
    height: 300px;
    border: 1px solid #CCC;
}
</style>

<div id="canvas"></div>
<div id="output"></div>

<script>
    var w = document.getElementById("canvas").offsetWidth;
    document.getElementById("output").innerHTML = w;
</script>
```

See this code live on jsFiddle (*http://jsfiddle.net/raphaeljs/9J37k/*).

It's very common for viewers using smartphones or tablets to rotate the device to get a better view, so we want to detect the width when this happens. In native JavaScript, you can do this using the `onsize` event listener attached to the global `window` variable:

```
function resize() {
    var w = document.getElementById("canvas").offsetWidth;
    document.getElementById("output").innerHTML = w + "<br />" +
        document.getElementById("output").innerHTML;
}
// page load
resize();

window.onresize = function() {
    // also fire on resize of page
    resize();
}
```

See this code live on jsFiddle (*http://jsfiddle.net/raphaeljs/9J37k/3/*).

Now the width of the container is measured both right away and whenever the page resizes. You can test this functionality in a browser by manually resizing the browser window with the mouse.

Assigning a function to window.onresize overwrites other functions already attached to this event, which can cause problems on pages using other libraries as well. It's best to use jQuery or at least be very mindful of what else might be sensitive to page resizing.

Let's put some stuff on the page to experiment with:

```
var paper = Raphael("canvas", 200, 200);

for (var c = 0; c < 20; c += 1) {
    paper.rect(c * 10, c * 10, 10, 10).attr("fill", "hsl(" + Math.random() + ",
0.5,0.5)");
}
```

Our goal here is to resize the objects dynamically to fit their container. Now that we have the width of that container, along with a function that conveniently fires every time that width changes, we could pretty easily use the transform method to do this. But that requires locating every object on the canvas, or at least dutifully placing each one in a global set of objects, which requires more tedious coding. As always, there's a better way.

We're going to use two methods of the paper object here: .setSize(), which adjusts the size of the paper object, and .setViewBox(), which adjusts the size of objects on that paper. The former is straightforward, but the latter requires a little bit of explanation.

Imagine the objects that you create with Raphael painted on the surface of a balloon that has been stretched a moderate amount. To resize them all at once, you might stretch out that balloon more, thus taking up a larger overall amount of area, or ease the tension to shrink them, thus taking up less area. The viewBox in the SVG specifications functions like this balloon.

Setting the viewBox to the *native size of the objects*—whatever area they take up before any transformations—then adjusting the size of the canvas functions like the easing or stretch of the balloon. Observe:

```
var paper = Raphael("canvas", 200, 200);

for (var c = 0; c < 20; c += 1) {
    paper.rect(c * 10, c * 10, 10, 10).attr("fill", "hsl(" + Math.random() + ",
0.5,0.5)");
}

// viewbox takes (x, y, w, h);
paper.setViewBox(0, 0, 200, 200);

function resize() {
    var w = document.getElementById("canvas").offsetWidth;
    paper.setSize(w, w);
```

```
    }

    resize();
    window.onresize = function() {
        resize();
    }
```

Now that we have this `resize` function set up, we're going to use a Raphael method called `.setSize()` to dynamically resize the canvas:

```
    function resize() {
        var w = document.getElementById("canvas").offsetWidth;
        paper.setSize(w, 200);
    }
```

See this code live on jsFiddle (*http://jsfiddle.net/raphaeljs/8r8tk/*).

Fire that up and drag the browser to differnt sizes and you'll see the 20 blocks we just made resize along with it.

Of course, you could easily add constraints to the `resize` function that prevent it from getting absurdly small. But the browser will handle it even if you don't.

Responsive design is a rich and complex subject, but at its core it's about moving and resizing things on the page according to the room they're given. The simple code here gets you 90% of the way. The other 10% is up to you.

Raphael in Every Context

We have begun every example in this book so far with some variation on the same line of code:

```
    var paper = Raphael("canvas", 500, 500);
```

We've always either referred to a large `<div>` element or placed the canvas object directly into the DOM. Now I'd like to show you an example of how to make Raphael blend in with other elements on the page.

Let's say we have a logo for a restaurant called "Paper Moon," for which we want to replace the vowels in "moon" with actual little moons.

First, we'll make a function to draw the shape of the moon, taking as an argument the phase from zero to one. (Technically, the moon appears to wax and wane from different directions (*http://bit.ly/moon-phase*), but here at Paper Moon we're more concerned with fine cuisine than with astronomical accuracy. But I invite you to fix it.)

```
    function shape(phase) {
        phase = typeof phase === "number" ? phase : 0.25;
        // limit phase to [0,1]
        phase = Math.max(0, Math.min(1, phase));
        // convert to [-1,1]
```

```
    phase = (phase - 0.5) * 2;

    // left arc
    var path = "M" + opts.r + ",0";
    path += "a" + opts.r + "," + opts.r + " 0 0,0 0," + opts.r * 2;

    var clockwise_flag = phase > 0 ? 0 : 1;
    phase = Math.abs(phase);

    // avoid divide by zero
    phase = phase || 0.0001;

    opts.inner_r = opts.r / Math.pow(phase, 0.5);

    path += "M" + opts.r + "," + opts.r * 2;
    path += "a" + opts.inner_r + "," + opts.inner_r + " 0 0," + clockwise_flag
+ " 0," + opts.r * -2;
    return path;
}
```

Next, let's make a function that makes a moon and returns an object. For good measure, we'll return it with a method for changing the phase of said moon after it is instantiated.

```
function moon(opts) {
    opts = opts || {};

    // set defaults (using ternary if/else statements)
    opts.r = typeof opts.r === "number" ? opts.r : 100;
    opts.phase = typeof opts.phase === "number" ? opts.phase : 0.25;
    opts.x = typeof opts.x === "number" ? opts.x : 0;
    opts.y = typeof opts.y === "number" ? opts.y : 0;

    if (opts.el && typeof opts.el === "string") {
        var paper = Raphael(opts.el, opts.r * 2, opts.r * 2);
    } else {
        var paper = Raphael(0, 0, opts.r * 2, opts.r * 2);
    }

    var shadow = paper.circle(opts.r + opts.x, opts.r + opts.y, opts.r).attr({
        'stroke-width': 0,
        fill: '#999'
    });

    function shape(phase) {
        // see above
    }

    var orb = paper.path(shape(opts.phase)).attr({
        'stroke-width': 0,
        stroke: "#999",
        fill: "#FF9"
    }).transform("T" + opts.x + "," + opts.y);
```

```
        return {
            setPhase: function(new_phase) {
                orb.attr("path", shape(new_phase));
            }
        }
    }
```

Okay. Try it out if you don't believe me.

To make the logo, we could use Raphael's .text() function to draw all the letters other than the two O's. But I don't particularly like text in the SVG specifications because it's such a pain to manually space everything out. We would need to figure out the distance that the two moons occupy and then resume the "n" in "moon" at exactly the right place. If only we had a technology that could snap to fit text on the page and take care of all the spacing itself.

Wait, we do! It's called HTML. Instead of rendering the entire logo in Raphael, we can make most of it the old-fashioned way. Unlike previous examples, we're going to use a <span> as the container for the canvas, meaning that it will display inline next to the letters.

```
<style>
.sign {
    background-color: darkblue;
    width: 375px;
    padding-left: 25px;
}

.sign span {
    color: silver;
    font-family: "Arial";
    font-size: 48px;
}
</style>

<div class="sign">
    <span>PAPER M</span>
    <span id="canvas1"></span>
    <span id="canvas2"></span>
    <span>N</span>
</div>

<script>
var m = moon({
    el: "canvas1",
    r: 18,
    phase: 0.75
});

var m = moon({
    el: "canvas2",
```

```
    r: 18,
    phase: 0.75
});
</script>
```

PAPER M●N

Ta-da! I would eat here every day. (There is actually a restaurant called Paper Moon where I live, but all I remember about it is that I spilled tomato sauce on my tie.)

See this code live on jsFiddle (*http://jsfiddle.net/raphaeljs/RbB4k/*).

Stealth Raphael

The above example may seem like a laborious way to demonstrate that Raphael can accept the `id` of a `<span>` element when at this point you probably would have taken my word for it. But I want to use our Moon Generator to demostrate a few other useful ways to make Raphael work for you.

You may have noticed that I built a little flexibility into the `opts.el` parameter. If a user passes a string, it uses that string as the ID of the element to house the `paper` object. If it's not a string or not present, we append the paper object to the DOM.

There's one more addition I'd like to make: allowing users—whether they be other humans with whom we share code or merely our future selves—to pass a pre-existing Raphael object.

The `paper` object is just that—an "object," as you can see by adding a `console.log(type of paper);` somewhere in your code. But a lot of things are objects, so we ought to test to see if what the user passed is really a Raphael object.

If you log the paper object to the screen, you'll see it has a property named `canvas`. That seems unique enough:

```
if (opts.el && typeof opts.el === "string") {
    var paper = Raphael(opts.el, opts.r * 2, opts.r * 2);
} else if (opts.el && typeof opts.el === "object" && opts.el.canvas) {
    var paper = opts.el;
} else {
    var paper = Raphael(0, 0, opts.r * 2, opts.r * 2);
}
```

This way, we can make lots of moons on the same canvas, like one of those really expensive watches (it's amazing what inspiration one can find in in-flight magazines).

```
var paper = Raphael("canvas", 500, 40);
```

```
for (var c = 0; c <= 1; c += 0.1) {
    var m = moon({
        el: paper,
        r: 20,
        phase: c,
        x: c * 420,
        y: 0
    });
}
```

See this code live on jsFiddle (*http://jsfiddle.net/raphaeljs/Mqzu7/*).

What this also means is that, because the function falls back on making its own canvas object, invoking it doesn't even require knowing that Raphael exists. If you were to distribute my moon function—and feel free to, it's all yours—other people can use it without reading this book... Though they really ought to.

That said, they'll still need to include the `raphael.js` script in the page before this function will work. Let's talk about ways to make that a little easier.

Raphael Plus Require.js, Browserify, or Another AMD Framework

For small projects like my modest (and fictional) restaurant, it's not really a big deal to just add a `<script src=raphael.js></script>` line.

In fact, Raphael is small enough—about 90Kb—that, if you use some sort of content management system that automatically adds the same header to every page, you can include Raphael in every page without much a performance hit to pages that don't need it. (Most modern browsers and servers automatically compress files, so it's typically much smaller.)

Still, most people will tell you that, for any sufficiently large site, every byte counts. Additionally, most large sites, like news publications or large retailers, probably have a lot of other JavaScript libraries firing off—those that track page views, those that serve advertisements, etc. The person in charge of overall site performance and stability, if it's not you, is probably not a person who's happy to toss any old library onto the page just because you read a book about it.

One of the main concerns in these situations is that the library will contribute global variables to the page that will accidentally overwrite other global variables from other libraries. This is one of the biggest difficulties in large-scale JavaScript development today. Because it was not designed to be a highly "module" language, with easy ways to drawn in libraries as you need them (the way you might in Python or NodeJS), you're playing with fire if you start mixing and matching a lot of third-party code.

Raphael has a small global footprint, so it's pretty safe. But to be extra cautious, you can use it's "ninja" mode to condense it all into one global variable, `Raphael`. Other libraries, like jQuery, call this "no conflict" mode. I can only hope "ninja" is a nod to the red-banded Teenage Mutant Ninja Turtle of the same name as this library.

In ninja mode, you wrap all of your Raphael code in a closure and pass that function the library itself:

```
(function (local_raphael) {
    var paper = local_raphael(10, 10, 320, 200);
    …
})(Raphael.ninja());
```

This function fires once when the page is ready, and whatever you do inside of it is protected from whatever other disasters your webmaster has inflicted on the global JavaScript environment.

RequireJS

If you use RequireJS to load external libraries—something that's a bit outside our scope here—you're probably used to ugly hacks to get libraries to work in that environment. Raphael is ready for you. It has a line in the source code to check for the presence of RequireJS and load itself correctly for use in that environment.

Browserify

I have recently become a convert to Browserify (*http://browserify.org/*), a Node.js module that allows one to include modules as though he or she were writing Node, a server-side implementation of JavaScript that has taken the scene by storm in past several years. After doing so, you run a simple command line statement to wrap all of the code—the Raphael source, your own code, and anything else you included—into one compressed file to include on your page. This eliminates the need to manually include the `ra phael.js` file on the page.

When you install Node, it comes prepackaged with a command line tool called `npm` ("node packaged modules") for painless installation of third-party code. To install Raphael as a node module, you would enter this command:

```
npm install raphael
```

This will download the Raphael source code as a module that is correctly packaged for use in Node (meaning it has a few extra JSON files pointing Node in the right direction). Your code will then look like this:

```
var Raphael = require("raphael");
var paper = Raphael(0, 0, 500, 500);
var circle = paper.circle(100, 100, 50);
```

After saving this file as something like code.js, you would run this:

```
browserify code.js > script.js
```

The script.js file now contains the Raphael source code and the above. As a bonus, it automatically runs inside a function, so circle, paper, and whatever else you declare will not find their way into the global namespace.

Final Thoughts: The Future of Raphael and You

As recently as July 2013, Raphael creator Dmitry Baranovskiy (whom I do not know personally) tweeted (*http://bit.ly/dmitry-tweet*) that he is still working on Raphael and that future versions are forthcoming. If you poke around on the Github repository for the project, you can see active development and bug fixes.

At the same time, Baranovskiy, who works for Adobe, is also working on a very similar library called Snap.svg (*http://snapsvg.io/*), which leaves behind support for old browsers in favor of the extra capabilities of modern ones. If you look at the sample code for Snap, you will see that it is nearly identical to Raphael.

Even though D3 has carved out a respectable place as the premier library for complex SVG graphics, I have no qualms about continuing to use Raphael for everything that is covered in this book and more. This is both for practical reasons—the IE8 holdouts will continue to cling to that awful browser for years to come—and because it is elegant and easy.

There's one other reason: Raphael makes drawing on the page easy, but not so easy that you don't still get a little paint on your fingers. There's an almost ineffable joy in fiddling with code, refreshing the browser, and being surprised—sometimes even pleasantly—by the result. I have never found an environment where the connection between one's ideas and the output is so thin and natural. Coding is turning ideas into instructions. I hope this book has given you enough command of the latter that you can explore the former to your heart's content.

About the Author

Chris Wilson is a journalist and developer at Time.com. Prior to joining the magazine, he was a "visual columnist" at Yahoo News and a senior editor at Slate, where he founded Slate Labs, which won the 2010 Ad Age Media Vanguard Award. He is a 2005 graduate of the University of Virginia and lives with his wife Susan in Washington, D.C.

Colophon

The animal on the cover of *RaphaelJS* is a Nile Valley Sunbird (*Hedydipna metallica*), a colorful passerine (perching) bird that is commonly found in the Middle East and northern Africa. Every February, the male Sunbird grows "nuptial plumage," which are vibrantly colored feathers that he displays to impress the females of the species.

The nuptial plumage tends to consist of glossy green/blue/violet feathers on the back and sides with a brilliant yellow underbelly and one or two long tail streamers. This is in stark opposition to the normal appearance of males and the year-round appearance of females: a musty brown body with a cream and dull-yellow colored belly and short tail. The mating display occurs for days, with the male being careful to display his plumage to the female and gain her attention through short calls that grow louder as the day continues. The male's bright plumage starts to fade after two to three months, and then the two sexes become almost physically indistinguishable.

Sunbirds require good sources of nectar, and are similar to hummingbirds in their feeding behaviors—they are quite small (only 15cm long at their largest) so they can dart and flicker around very quickly, and even have a hummingbird-like beak that is best suited to trumpet-shaped flowers. Although the Nile Valley Sunbird population has not been officially quantified, it has been designated as stable because of the frequency of sightings and the birds' large range of habitat. Sunbirds are best known for being frequent visitors to the famous walled gardens of Oman, Yemen, Saudi Arabia, and Egypt.

The cover image is from Meyers' *Kleines Lexikon*. The cover fonts are URW Typewriter and Guardian Sans. The text font is Adobe Minion Pro; the heading font is Adobe Myriad Condensed; and the code font is Dalton Maag's Ubuntu Mono.

Get even more for your money.

Join the O'Reilly Community, and register the O'Reilly books you own. It's free, and you'll get:

- $4.99 ebook upgrade offer
- 40% upgrade offer on O'Reilly print books
- Membership discounts on books and events
- Free lifetime updates to ebooks and videos
- Multiple ebook formats, DRM FREE
- Participation in the O'Reilly community
- Newsletters
- Account management
- 100% Satisfaction Guarantee

Signing up is easy:

1. Go to: oreilly.com/go/register
2. Create an O'Reilly login.
3. Provide your address.
4. Register your books.

Note: English-language books only

To order books online:
oreilly.com/store

For questions about products or an order:
orders@oreilly.com

To sign up to get topic-specific email announcements and/or news about upcoming books, conferences, special offers, and new technologies:
elists@oreilly.com

For technical questions about book content:
booktech@oreilly.com

To submit new book proposals to our editors:
proposals@oreilly.com

O'Reilly books are available in multiple DRM-free ebook formats. For more information:
oreilly.com/ebooks

O'REILLY®

Spreading the knowledge of innovators | oreilly.com

Have it your way.

www.ingramcontent.com/pod-product-compliance
Ingram Content Group UK Ltd.
Pitfield, Milton Keynes, MK11 3LW, UK
UKHW030727220525
458817UK00008B/251